Shark Beneath the Reef

Jean Craighead George

••••

With

Connected Readings

PRENTICE HALL
Upper Saddle River, New Jersey
Needham, Massachusetts

ISBN 0-13-437498-3

3 4 5 6 7 8 9 10 03 02 01 00

PRENTICE HALL

Acknowledgments

Grateful acknowledgment is made to the following for copyrighted material:

Evil Eye Music, Inc.
"The Silver Fish" from *Where the Sidewalk Ends* by Shel Silverstein. Copyright © 1974 Evil Eye Music, Inc. Published by HarperCollins Publishers. Reprinted by permission of Evil Eye Music, Inc.

Farrar, Straus & Giroux
"Plumed Serpent in Tula" from *The Serpent and the Sun* retold by Cal Roy. Copyright © 1972 by Calvin L. Roy. All rights reserved. Reprinted by permission of Farrar, Straus & Giroux.

Harcourt Brace & Company
"Eugenie Clark and the Sleeping Sharks" from *Wild Animals, Gentle Women,* copyright © 1978 by Margery Facklam, reprinted by permission of Harcourt Brace & Company.

HarperCollins Publishers
Shark Beneath the Reef by Jean Craighead George. Copyright © 1989 by Jean Craighead George. Used by permission of HarperCollins Publishers.

Houghton Mifflin Company
"The Poor Boy Was Wrong" from *The Hopeful Trout and Other Limericks* by John Ciardi. Text copyright © 1989 by Myra J. Ciardi. Reprinted by permission of Houghton Mifflin Company.

Raintree Children's Books
"Sharks: The Perfect Hunters" from *Sharks and Troubled Waters* by Margaret Harris. Copyright © 1977 by Contemporary Perspectives, Inc.

(Acknowledgments continue on p. 159.)

Contents

Shark Beneath the Reef

Shark Beneath the Reef

Jean Craighead George

A Round, Black Eye

A *THUMP* and *kersplash* awoke Tomás Torres. He blinked his eyes and listened. *Thump, kersplash.* It was five A.M. His pelican alarm clock was going off. The brown pelicans were up. They were diving into the sea in the blue darkness, plunging headfirst to scoop up fish in their enormous beaks with nets of skin. On the fourth *kersplash* Tomás rolled to his feet. Yawning, he stepped naked from the *palapa,* an architectural wonder of *palo blanco* tree posts gracefully roofed and walled with palm leaves. He heard the deep, soft breathing of his grandfather and uncle, still asleep on the sandy floor of their airy *palapa* house.

Tomás strode out of the palm porch and looked from the island of Coronados, where he stood, across the Sea of Cortez to the peninsula of Baja California, Mexico, a mountain range in the sea that is the toe of the Rockies. The mountains stretched north and south from horizon to horizon, and in the low light they looked like a gargantuan cutout of a jaw of shark's teeth. Above them stars shone as bright as fire. The sun would not be up for an hour. Tomás ran down the white coral beach to the water.

"Good morning," he called to the pelicans. Wading up to his waist, he took a breath and dived into water as clear as air. With the grace of a sea lion Tomás sped through a crowd of awakening fish that were beginning to school up for the day. Near the bottom he rolled onto his back and looked up. Above him darted a flock of little diving birds. They swam in spurts and dashes as they chased fish. Tomás shot to the surface.

"Excuse me!" he said to the tidy eared grebes as he exploded into their midst. Unabashed, the small loonlike birds swam closer to him. "Go home to your pools in the United States," he said. "This is my cove."

Tomás laughed from his belly to his eyes, a laugh so joyful it often turned people's heads to see who could be so happy. He lunged to catch a grebe. When it dived, he began counting. The bird did not pop up to breathe for two whole minutes.

"I wish I could stay down as long as you can," he said as the grebe paddled toward him, head underwater, looking for fish.

When it dived again, Tomás swam with it into the night-filled depths of the cove waters.

One, two, three, he began. At fifty-five he burst to the surface. The bird was still underwater. "If I could hold my breath as long as you," he went on, "I could catch the whale shark my uncle saw, the one that tore my grandfather's net." The net lay on the beach not far from the *palapa*, like a cobweb torn by an eagle. Tomás flipped onto his back and kicked toward shore.

I would jab him in the heart, he thought, and bring him up on my spear. I can do it. I will carry the shark above my head through the streets of Loreto. The mission bells will ring. The padre will say, "Good has won over evil." The fishermen of Loreto will sing, "Tomás is brave. Tomás is strong. He killed the net ripper." The fishermen will dance and sing and feast for ten days and ten nights.

Sucking in a mouthful of water, he squirted it high in the air, then rolled to his stomach and stabbed an imaginary shark.

I can get him, his thoughts went on, because the monster isn't a killer shark. He's a whale shark. Uncle Miguel saw him come up out of the deep water where whale sharks live. He saw him swim toward Coronados Island. Whale sharks are slow and dumb. They can't even catch a sea slug. I'll spear him easily.

A round eye as black as the center of the earth peered through the clear water at him. It hung near the indigo edge of the rock reef and was separated from the other eye by three feet of cartilage, muscle and skin. Tomás's scent traveled to the smelling lobe of the brain through nostrils located under the eyes. The scent of hundreds of terrified fish also traveled to that brain. The sound of Tomás's kicking was received through the skin and the nerves on either side of the long dark body. The round, black eye enlarged and quivered with excitement.

Tomás did not know he was targeted. He was lying on his back, kicking with his feet, sculling with his hands and daydreaming.

In his dream he was carrying the shark into the plaza in front of the old mission in his hometown of Loreto, once the capital of Baja California. Tomás's small, compact body moved gracefully in his dream suit of spun gold. He wore a helmet decorated with the long gold feathers of the quetzal bird. It was a helmet like Quetzalcoatl's, Tomás's hero and a god-hero of the ancient Aztec and Toltec Indians of Mexico.

Quetzalcoatl, he called in his dream. Help me lift the shark.

Although Tomás Torres went to the Catholic church, the gods of his Indian past were still very real to him and his family. He was, like most Mexicans, a mestizo, part Spanish and part Indian. And although Spanish was his native language and Spain his motherland, Tomás's memory—like that of his fellow mestizos—did not begin with the arrival of the Spanish in Mexico. It went back to the glorious Mexican past, when gods of good and evil reigned and warriors were eagles, jaguars and feathered serpents—to a time when Mexico was young and ambitious.

Tomás kicked toward the white beach, racing away from the dark water where the eye watched him. He was playing a game with his past, racing from dark to light, from evil to good. The beach was good. It was bright and white, like Quetzalcoatl. The dark waters behind him were like Tezcatlipoca, the evil man who drove Quetzalcoatl from the ancient Toltec Indian capital to wander and die.

Tomás's spine tingled. He loved the sensation of racing from evil to good, and as he shivered with excitement, the round eye lined him up with its companion eye, and Tomás was in focus.

He put his feet down on the white sea bottom and was safe. Tilting back his head, he stared at the planet Venus, now low in the sky. It was as big as the moon and as white as a diamond. This, the morning star, his grandfather had told him, was the heart of Quetzalcoatl. When this Toltec leader, who had discovered corn and invented science, agriculture and the calendar, died in exile, he was consumed by divine fire. His ashes became the birds, and his heart the sparkling Venus. Tomás kept his eye on the morning star.

I'll find the great shark, Quetzalcoatl, he vowed. Then you'll come down and help me vanquish him.

You are going to return. You said so.

And I'll recognize you. I won't make the same mistake Montezuma did. He thought Hernán Cortés was you, and his warriors your hosts. He gave you gold to appease you, hoping to send you back to the birds. But Cortés and his men hungered for gold and more gold. War broke out and the great leaders died. The beautiful temples crumbled away.

I shall not make the same mistake, Quetzalcoatl, he decided. You are a feathered serpent. Grandpapa has seen you coming down the mountain to drink in the sea.

The round eye did not unfocus on the body that was kicking and sculling at the edge of the beach. The body's scent, sound and shape were too exciting as they traveled from the eye, the nostril and the skin to the brain. There they triggered the feeding frenzy. The shark writhed.

Tomás went on dreaming.

"Lady of Guadalupe," he called. "I need you, too. I need all the help I can get to kill this shark."

It did not seem strange to Tomás that he was calling on two histories, the history of the Mexicans before the Spanish conquest and the history after. The Lady of Guadalupe was also an important part of his life. She was modern and peculiarly Mexican. She had appeared only a few hundred years ago to a humble mestizo peasant on a dry, dusty road. The mother of Jesus asked the humble man to go to the bishop and request that a mission be built on the spot where she stood. After many years and as many requests, the peasant finally convinced the bishop he had seen a miracle. The mission was built, and the Lady of Guadalupe became the hope of millions of hardworking peasants, laborers and fishermen—Mexico's poor. Tomás called on the Lady of Guadalupe to help with his quest just as freely as he had called upon Quetzalcoatl. They were very much alike. Both were good.

The water darkened behind him.

Tomás kicked again, and his back touched sand. He sat up on the beach and heard, far out in the darkness, an armada of boats speeding northward toward the fishing grounds at the tip of Coronados Island.

"The gringos are coming," he said. The Mexican fishing guides were taking the sportfishermen—largely wealthy Americans—out to catch the big-game fish of December—cabrilla, pompano, sierra, snapper, tuna and yellowtail. In other months they went after silvery amberjacks, dark-blue dolphins, marlins and groupers. Loreto was a world-famous fishing ground, and sportsmen descended upon it all year round. Tomás and his family, who were commercial shark fishermen, considered the sportfishermen amusing visitors who brought dollars and jobs to Loreto, but who were no threat to their own fishing.

Tomás splashed his face and ran his fingers through his thick, black hair. Droplets ran off his straight nose and ruddy cheeks. His eyes were wide apart and very black. Water clung to his long dark lashes.

His morning bath done, he rocked in the small waves at the edge of the sea and summoned back his imaginary whale shark. The round yellow spots that made this shark different from all other sharks shone like fiery jewels between the prominent ridges on its body. He saw the cavernous mouth that swept up tons of plankton as the monster rushed through the deep waters of the Sea of Cortez. He saw the mouth fall open in death.

This, the biggest fish in the world, which often grew to be forty-five feet, was not a killer shark. It had no teeth.

The whale shark was valuable. Its skin was fashioned into leather goods more durable and beautiful than pigskin. The fins were brewed into the rare and exotic shark-fin soup, and the delicious meat was sold to the gourmet restaurants in Mexico City. It was unusual to have a whale shark off the shores of Loreto, for its natural home was deep in the sea, and the very mystery of its presence inspired Tomás's imagination.

He dreamed on. Now he was looking into his shark's lidless eye. It glowed like the sun rising out of the sea. A tear welled up. Tomás felt a sudden tenderness for the great fish. In his mind he threw the shark backward over his head and turned to watch it fall. As it struck the water it *kersplash*ed and turned into a pelican. He stopped dreaming. The sun was up.

Tomás ran up the beach of white coral sand and past the fish-cleaning table and jumped over the damaged net. It was stretched out on the sand to dry so it could be repaired. The Tórreses had two big shark nets. The other was set in the sea between Coronados and Carmen islands. Ramón and Miguel checked it twice a day. Tomás helped them when school was out, as it was now for the two-week Christmas festival. On most weekends and in the summer he lived in the island *palapa*, amusing himself by diving to watch the reef fish and helping Ramón and Miguel with the heavy nets. Seeing no possibility of catching the whale shark today, Tomás thought of another plan. Stepping into the *palapa*, he took his shirt and trousers off a twig hook drilled into a strut, dressed and joined Ramón, who was preparing breakfast.

"Grandpapa," he said, "can I climb the volcano today?" Ramón's eyes twinkled. This was a game the two often played. The answer was always no followed by a vivid lecture that went like this:

"The climb is perilous. Rocks fall, eagles circle, vultures come to pick your bones. The evil Tezcatlipoca roars at you." Tomás would cringe, act terrified and—stay home.

Today his grandfather did not answer. The light of the rising sun illuminated his slender figure. Ramón Torres wore his trousers rolled to his knees. His bare feet were scarred and sunburned. He stood before the *palapa* kitchen, a table-high box filled with sand. On one end a very small fire burned, lighting the pots and cups neatly stacked at the other end.

"Can I climb the volcano?" Tomás repeated. Again Ramón did not answer, but the nostrils of his blunt, narrow nose flared slightly as if he were about to speak. He smiled, and his white teeth contrasted sharply with his rich brown skin. Tomás was his joy. He had happily loved and spoiled him since Tomás's father had died when Tomás was two years old. Ramón had protected him, as he had all his children, within the palm-leaf fences of his Loreto home. It was a half acre of grassless desert and *palapas* in the fishermen's colony of Loreto.

Tomás had two loves—school and fishing—and he liked them equally. They were sometimes at war with each other, for one demanded sitting still in wonder, and the other demanded action, albeit in wonder, too. Someday, he knew, he would have to decide between them, but until then he could enjoy them both. Life as Tomás was living it was wonderful. His mother and grandmother fussed over him, washing his clothes, feeding and praising him, and his grandfather saw to it that he never knew hunger. Ramón's half acre of desert was well stocked with the date palms, lemon, avocado, pomegranate and olive trees, the trees the Jesuit monks had introduced to Baja from Spain in the 1500s. Furthermore, Ramón was the most successful of the famous shark fishermen of Loreto. There had always been fish for his large family of thirteen, eleven of whom were now married and living in La Paz, the new capital of Baja. His two youngest sons, Miguel and Ramón Jr., Tomás's father, had stayed home to help Ramón. Shark fishing was strenuous work. It required two, and preferably three, strong men to pull the huge nets and drag in the heavy sharks. Furthermore, shark fishing was dangerous. Not only could violent storms strike the Sea of Cortez suddenly and disastrously, but the big man-eaters like the hammerheads and tiger sharks fought the men who were pulling them into the boats. At these times Ramón would warn Tomás to keep his distance. "Sharks die from the tail up," he would say, "and their jaws are the last to go."

Ramón kneaded a piece of cornmeal dough in the palm of his hand. He was remembering, as he often did, the huge hammerhead shark that in the frenzy of dying had slammed its vicious jaws on Ramón Jr.'s arm and chest. Before Ramón could cut away the net and get Tomás's father back to Loreto, Ramón Jr. had died from loss of blood.

Ramón lifted his eyes and looked across the water to the peninsula where Ramón Jr. lay long dreaming under the blue tile tomb in the graveyard. He believed his favorite son was sitting somewhere beyond the gauzy veil of death, waiting for him to come home from the island and bring him wine and fish. Like most mestizos, Ramón's understanding of life and death was more Aztec than Christian. To him neither birth nor death interrupted the flow of life. Babies were born. Men and women died, and more babies were born. In each stage of the cycle there was life. Ramón Jr. required food and drink and fresh clothes from time to time. On holidays and on the Day of the Dead, in November, Ramón and his wife, Dolores, and Tomás and his mother, Francisca, would picnic in the graveyard with Ramón Jr. and leave him food, wine and bright plastic flowers.

Ramón flattened the ball of dough between his palms and placed it on a round iron grill that stood on short legs above the fire.

"Yes, Tomás," he suddenly said. "You can."

Tomás startled. The answer had been so long in coming that he had forgotten what he had asked. When he did recall, he was dumbfounded.

"Really? I can climb the volcano?"

"Come and eat." Ramón flipped over the corn tortilla with his fingers, filled it with spiced fish and gave it to Tomás. He ate. Tomás always obeyed his grandfather if he heard him. Often he did not, especially when he was on some imaginary adventure, stabbing whale sharks or sailing the ship that Miguel had told him was wrecked on the top of Coronados volcano.

Savoring his fish tortilla, Tomás walked down the beach to join Miguel, who was scrubbing the inside of the big blue-and-white *ponga.*

"Tell me about the ship on the top of the volcano," he said.

"Yes, yes," began Miguel. "Many years ago, a fair-skinned Spaniard set sail from the Yucatán on the east coast of Mexico, in a ship laden with gold." He stopped talking.

"Then what?"

"You know the rest."

"Tell me again."

"He miraculously sailed over the land into the mysterious waters of the Sea of Cortez. There he and his ship disappeared."

Miguel looked up at the graceful volcano that was the island. From out at sea it resembled a rosy cone with sloping shoulders floating on the green-blue water. Coronados was an unusual island and very beautiful.

"If you look closely you can see the mast of the Spaniard's ship," Miguel said.

Tomás squinted. A golden shaft speared the sky. Sails billowed out, orders were shouted. The ship floundered and vanished. Tomás turned to his uncle.

"Tell me more."

"There is no more," Miguel said, bailing water now. "And stop asking. You always ask too many questions when you've been out here without playmates too long. Go find yourself a little lizard to talk to."

The three fishermen were alone on the island. Although tourists sometimes picnicked on the picturesque white beach, and an occasional commercial fisherman left his nets there for the day, only the Tórreses had a home on the island. Ramón had been fishing out of the *palapa* since he was twelve years old and newly arrived from the mainland. He had left the state of Sonora for Baja, where the fish were as abundant as sand grains. With his own hands he had also built a home in Loreto. Although he had never paid for it, the land was his. In Mexico a man owned the land he settled and lived upon.

As the sun appeared over the rim of the sea, the willets, terns and herons arrived on the beach in that order, each on its own light cue. Every bird species awakened at a different light threshold. In near darkness the pelicans got up. When the sun was higher, the willets and grebes appeared; then the terns, gulls and herons flew in. The last to fall out of the vanishing darkness were the sanderlings.

"Pow!" Tomás said to three tiny, long-legged birds that dropped from the sky and ran along the edge of the water like flickering sunlight.

"Pow! Hey, Miguel, look—magic. I say 'pow' and birds fall out of the sky.

"Pow! Pow!" Two more white-and-tan sanderlings dropped to the water's edge. They appeared so suddenly that it did seem like magic.

Miguel laughed. A sturdy, well-built young man with a fine black mustache and gentle eyes, he too loved Tomás. When his infant daughter and two-year-old son had died several years ago, he had adopted Tomás in his heart and thought of him as his own. He and his wife prayed for more children, but their prayers had not been answered, and so Miguel gave the great love for his own lost children to Tomás. Like most Mexican parents of young children, he had encouraged Tomás to dream and enjoy himself. All too soon, he knew, playtime would be over and childhood gone.

For Tomás the time was not far off. He would graduate from ninth grade at the end of this year. After that, by Mexican law he was free to leave school and go to work, or stay on and go to high school.

To fish or to study? Tomás would ask himself every now and then, then shake his head. The decision was painful.

"Be a fisherman," Miguel advised him one day. "You will never be unhappy or starve if you fish."

"But I love school, too," he would answer. Tomás had a young science teacher, Juan Fuertes, who took him into the desert and along the coast, showing him how the animals of Baja lived in the fiery and waterless desert. Tomás learned quickly and wished he knew more. But he also liked to fish—to sail out in the pale blue *ponga* with the wind in his hair and sea spray on his face. On the water he was as free as *águila,* the eagle, and *ballena,* the great whale that dived and sounded in the Sea of Cortez. One day he asked Ramón to help him decide what to do.

"Time and maturity will decide for you," he had said as he threaded a shuttle to mend a net—and Tomás suspected they would. But what and when? He was impatient for an answer.

The sandpipers ran back and forth hunting tiny crabs. Miguel stored two bottles of fresh water in the *ponga,* then challenged Tomás to a race to the *palapa.* They slid up to the table together.

"Miguel," Tomás said as he brushed off his pants, "I'm not going with you. Today I climb the volcano."

"No," Miguel answered emphatically. "It's too dangerous. Besides, Ramón says the *oficiales* are looking for fishermen. They may come here. Someone must meet them and find out what they want."

"The *oficiales*?" Tomás said apprehensively. "What could they want of us?"

"I do not know," said Miguel, frowning. "But *oficiales* always mean trouble."

"What do I do if they come?"

"Go climb the volcano," grunted Ramón, who had joined them.

"What will they do to us?" Tomás asked his grandfather.

"Nothing," he answered. "*Oficiales* do one thing one day and something else the next. Once they built a fine government restaurant in Loreto for no reason. A month later it was closed for no reason.

"Next the *oficiales* build a costly solar-powered seawater distillery. It irrigated the land for a month; and then it closed.

"*Oficiales* do not know what they want," he concluded.

Tomás looked at him quizzically. "Is this politics you are talking, Grandpapa?" he asked.

"Yes, it is politics," Ramón replied.

"You have never talked to me like this before."

"You are now fourteen—old enough to join the men's talk."

Tomás heard and was pleased. He threw out his chest and ran to the *ponga.*

"Get in, Grandpapa. Get in, Miguel," he said. "I'll push you off." The fishermen climbed aboard, and Tomás pressed his hands against the *ponga.* The muscles in his arms rose like the volcano as he shoved the boat into the water. He observed them with pleasure. He would soon be strong like Miguel. Perhaps he should be a fisherman.

Politics, he said to himself as he stepped back. Now that I am old enough to talk politics, how do I begin?

A Black Cross in the Sky

THE long, low-slung *ponga* sat rigid on the water. Neither Tomás's leaning on it nor the fishermen's energetic movements could rock the sturdy boat.

A brown pelican swam up to Ramón and eyed him hopefully, for he knew the generosity of this fisherman well.

"No food today, Boca Grande," Ramón said, showing the bird an empty hand.

"Want to know something?" Tomás was still hanging on to the *ponga*, trying to start a political conversation and wondering how to begin.

"Yes," answered Ramón.

"Well . . . " He could think of nothing political, and so he blurted out what he thought was really important.

"Boca Grande has chicks," he said.

"How do you know that?"

"Its head has white feathers, not yellow or brown like most of the pelicans. The white head and the black streak down the back of the neck say, 'I am feeding chicks.'"

"Where did you learn that?"

"I watched the pelicans at their roost," Tomás said. "The ones that looked like Boca Grande were feeding chicks. The yellow- and brown-headed ones were not. The science teacher said I am right."

"I've always wondered why pelicans came in three colors," said Miguel, looking at the chunky-bodied bird with new interest. Another pelican dropped headfirst into the water from thirty feet up, surfaced and swallowed a fish.

"A yellow head," said Tomás. "That one has no chicks. But it is an adult. The brown-headed ones are yearlings." Ramón was impressed with Tomás's knowledge. The boy really did like to learn.

Tomás shoved the *ponga* into deeper water so that Miguel could drop the outboard motor, an Evinrude 55 that was Ramón's pride and for which he had saved for seven years.

"Did you say you are not going to fish the Shallows today, Grandpapa?" Tomás asked, still holding on to the *ponga.*

"That's right," he answered. "We are going out to the deep basin off Carmen Island. We haven't caught much in the Shallows for a long time."

"Why is that? Are there too many fishermen?" Tomás was thinking of the armada of sportfishing boats that roared by every morning to fish the waters off Coronados Island. These men and women rarely took sharks, but Tomás knew they caught the fish that the killer sharks fed upon.

"Mostly it's the Japanese fish-factory boats," said Miguel.

Every fisherman in Loreto had despaired when the government had permitted the huge foreign factory boats to come into the Sea of Cortez several years ago. Like huge vacuum cleaners, the boats sucked up every living thing in their paths—game fish, sharks, squid, shrimp, even snails, shellfish and sea urchins. These were culled, and the fish canned or frozen aboard ship and taken to Japan for marketing.

"Why do they affect us?" Tomás asked. "The factory ships are far out in the sea. Our fish stay in our waters."

"That is so," Miguel said, tinkering with the motor. "But the factory ships kill all the baby fish. They kill baby sharks and squid and even baby coral and sponges. There are practically no little ones to grow up and replace the big ones we take. Our catch has been dropping off steadily since the factory boats came in."

"But the sea is endless, Miguel. You said so."

"Apparently it is not," he replied, checking the gas. "Apparently it is not."

"Why does our government let these boats suck up our fish?" Tomás asked, pleased to be, at last, talking politics.

"Money," Miguel said. "The Japanese pay the *oficiales* huge sums of money."

"But they are *our* fish." Tomás was truly upset.

"What can we do?" shrugged Miguel, settling himself beside the Evinrude. "Have another revolution? We've had two already. The first one to free us from Spain and the second to free us from the rich landlords. Did they help?"

Tomás thought about that. According to his social-studies book, the Revolution of 1910 and the new Constitution of 1917 had given the people many rights, as well as some needed land reforms. It was a good constitution. But when Tomás looked around Loreto, he saw that the poor were still poor and the rich were growing ever richer.

Miguel pulled the starter cord. The motor hummed, and Tomás let go of the boat.

"What should I do if the *oficiales* arrive?" he shouted as the boat backed away.

"Laugh for them," said Ramón.

"Bribe them," said Miguel. "That's how the system works."

"We don't have any money."

"Then it's too bad for us," said Miguel bitterly.

Tomás watched the blue-and-white *ponga* swing in an arc and speed toward the open sea. As it rounded the southern end of the cove, a dark body with a strange head shaped like an enormous mallet passed under the *ponga* on its way to the rock reef. The reef was the end of a dyke of volcanic lava that began high up on the mountain, ran down behind the *palapa* and jutted out three hundred feet into the sea. It formed the north end of the cove where the Tórreses camped.

Tomás stood alone, feeling the chill of awareness; and he did not like it. He did not like to know that the Japanese factory boats were sucking up his family's living. He did not like to know that the *oficiales* were coming to the island, probably to bring bad news.

He whistled to clear his head. But the problems would not go away. Ramón and Miguel had been bringing home less fish for the market. Grandmother Dolores was not buying fresh bakery bread and sugar cookies anymore—not even canned refried beans. Tomás squeezed his eyes closed and called upon his imagination for help. He saw the annual Christmas pageant at the Lady of Loreto Mission. In the play the forces of good—the warriors, hermits, nuns and angels—battled the forces of evil—the devils and bulls. After a long struggle good triumphed.

"And it does every year," Tomás said aloud to the sea, feeling better. "Everything is going to be sunshine." He turned a cartwheel and skipped a stone across the still water.

The rising sun had changed the sky-reflecting sea from night black to dawn gold. As the water changed, the Coronados volcano shifted from gray to pink, and the distant mountains turned hot violet-reed. The day was going to be very warm. Tomás plunked himself down in the chair his father had made long ago out of driftwood and turned his thoughts from politics to the volcano.

Now, how would a Spanish galleon get up there in the first place? he asked himself. Miguel must be wrong. The ship must be from a far earlier time, when the volcano was short and young like a baby. The ship docked on it and rose with the mountain into the sky. He squinted and saw the mast again, but it was not as bright a gold as Miguel claimed it to be.

That proves it is very ancient, he reasoned. It must be the boat Quetzalcoatl escaped in when the evil Tezcatlipoca tricked him into sinning and then forced him to flee.

A verdin, a little songbird, flew past Tomás, carrying a strand of grass for one of the many ball-shaped nests in which he roosted out of the hot blazing sun of summer and was protected from the torrential tropical rains of winter. Tomás called these nests "bird *palapas*" and usually followed the little verdins to see how they wove their hollow balls; but not today. The ship was the quest he had chosen.

It has to be Quetzalcoatl's ship, he concluded, and jumped to his feet. And now to find it.

Tomás put on the Nike shoes his mother had given him for his fourteenth birthday. He was proud of them, for they were very fashionable. They had Velcro straps instead of laces and were the colors of Mexico's flag—red, white and green.

He rolled down his trouser legs so the thorn bushes would not scratch him and filled his canteen with drinking water from the big plastic drum. Since there was no fresh water on Coronados, except in one pool after a hard rain, the Tórreses brought their water to the island. Tomás screwed on the canteen lid, stuffed the leftover cooked fish into his pocket and started off.

The trail began in an arroyo, a dry streambed that came down the volcano's slope. Even at its beginning the path was a fortress. The stiff, spiny limbs of the mesquite and the elastic twigs of the elephant trees were entwined like a bale of barbed wire. When he tried to progress, thorns tore his clothing and leathery limbs bounced him backward. He was forced to cut his way with his knife.

Farther along, huge stands of old-man's beard and spiny cholla cacti pushed him back. He circled them, wedged between boulders and finally scrambled up out of the arroyo onto a barren plateau of rocks and scattered plants.

Here the trail ended, and Tomás sat down to rest and search for a route up the barren cone. His eyes wandered across the vast panorama before him. Across the jade-green sea stood the Baja California mountains. In the full light of the sun they were not cardboard cutouts but massive structures, deeply eroded and partially forested with huge cardón cacti forty feet high. In their arroyos grew the graceful thatch palm of the *palapas*, the Washington palm.

They are not charming mountains. No lakes or rivers glitter on their landscape. They are tough, cruel mountains, dry and hostile. They drive off intruders. The conquistadors, early monks and padres deserted them soon after finding them. U.S. generals and developers came, saw and returned to their sweeter homelands. The Baja California mountains are raw and hot and strong, and Tomás loved them.

About three million years ago this mountain range created the Sea of Cortez when it broke off from the mainland of Mexico and drifted into the Pacific Ocean on one of the earth's sliding crusts. The range is Baja, Mexico. Two million years later, hot magnum spewed up from the sea floor and volcanic islands appeared. One of these, and to Tomás the most beautiful of all the desert islands near Loreto, was Coronados.

Looking down through eagle eyes, one would see that Coronados Island is shaped like a turtle. It rises almost a thousand feet above the surface of the sea. Its sloping shoulders are sparsely thicketed, its summit practically barren of life, but underwater the rocks of Coronados are an Eden. An upwelling of cold, nutrient-rich waters feeds reef fishes and sea creatures of a million designs and colors. The reefs were Tomás's world. He dived to them whenever he could. Along the reefs he did not have to dream. Nature's incredible living dreams swam and crept all around him.

Now, high above the reefs, Tomás stared down on the cool green of the Sea of Cortez and wished he were in it. He was hot, rapidly losing interest in the ship and about to turn back.

A fishing boat appeared in the sky. He blinked. It soared above the water as thin and vulnerable as a dragonfly, then shimmered and vanished. Tomás rubbed his eyes.

"Mirage," he said. The boat reappeared.

"Maybe that's how the ship got to the top of the volcano," he mused. "It floated up in a mirage and never came down. There has to be some good reason."

Inspired by this thought, he began climbing. Above him the volcano warped and bent in the air ripples created by the ninety-degree heat, and again his resolve faded.

But I can't go back, he thought. If Miguel is right and the ship is gold, Grandpapa will not have to worry about the factory boats or the *oficiales* ever again.

He put one foot on an enormous boulder, then the other, balanced, scrambled to the top of the rock slide and rested. A gnatcatcher, a pretty little island bird, darted over his head and alighted on a spiny twig. It sang, then flew up the mountain.

The bird is showing me the way, he thought, and followed it over an avalanche of rocks to a steep wall. Fluttering on the wing, the gnatcatcher darted here and there frantically, then flew down the mountain.

A warning, Tomás said to himself. Now the bird is telling me to go back. He listened, expecting to hear Tezcatlipoca roar.

Heat waves shimmered off the hot rocks—he heard a scream.

Clutching his heart, Tomás looked up. *Aguila*, the osprey, was overhead, calling to his mate as he carried a snakelike needlefish toward his island nest. Tomás laughed at himself. He knew that call well, but here on the side of the barren volcano, searching for a ship of gold, the sea eagle had sounded like a demon.

Tomás joked to himself and inched up a hot wall until he came out on a plateau of broken rocks and spiny grasses. Sitting down, he opened his canteen and drank. The cove below was a cool, blue-green jewel, and he took in its freshness with his eyes, then considered the volcano again.

From where he sat, he could see no obvious route up the cone, so he simply got to his feet and climbed. Up, he said to himself, is a route itself.

A rock slipped under his foot. He flattened against a boulder. The rock plunged down the mountain, hit, bounced and fell on. It set other rocks crashing and rolling, splintering and avalanching. They piled onto the spot where he had just sipped his water. Their roar and dust settled into silence. Fear tingled through Tomás's veins. He knew he should go back. Grandpapa was right, the volcano was too dangerous to climb.

But I must find the ship and the gold, he resolved, and scrambled on and up. A boulder wobbled under his feet. Quickly he jumped to another, then another. Like a fly he walked up the hot incline, climbing on and on, not daring to look down. Lizards ran out of their dens, crossed in front of his face and disappeared into the cracks.

Finally he went over a wall and clambered onto a ledge. He gasped. A forum of demons was staring at him, their shoulders hunched up over their naked heads, their claws scratching the rocks.

"Tezcatlipocas, what do you want?" he whispered hoarsely. The circle of devils had red-rimmed eyes set in skin-covered skulls. One walked toward him. A ruff of feathers around its neck lifted and fell back. Slowly it unfolded black wings until they expanded six feet from tip to tip. The hot, rising air lifted them, and the creature soared upward and backward. Another floated off in this manner, then all of them.

"Vultures," Tomás said with relief, and climbed on.

After a long scramble he sighted the rim of the crater and, using hands and feet, scaled a gritty wall, reached another plateau and rested. A black shadow crossed his hand, and he looked up to see a vulture attacking. The hooked beak opened, and partially digested carrion spewed out. Foul smelling, it splattered on the rocks. Tomás almost threw up.

Tezcatlipoca is defending the mountain with vultures, he thought. Grandpapa is right. I'm going back.

Tomás turned to go down. In looking for a place to set his foot, he saw two large, speckled eggs lying on the bare ground.

"A nest," he said aloud. "A turkey vulture's nest. The bird is defending it. It is not sent by Tezcatlipoca." Tomás laughed and wiped his sweaty head. "On I go," he said, and climbed.

On the next plateau he spotted a chimneylike groove that led to the top, and set out for that.

The vultures dived at him again and again, but now he could enjoy them. They were not devils, but the old friends he saw every day circling the island. They were simply defending their nests and eggs.

At the chimney he placed his hands and feet against the walls and, moving cautiously, not daring to look down, moved up and up until, perspiring and tired, he finally made the top. He crawled on hands and knees to the edge of the sun-blackened crater and looked down.

"There's no ship!" he cried. "There's no ship!"

After a long time he rocked to his heels, opened his canteen and took a drink.

"I should never have come," Tomás said aloud. "Miguel was right." Tomás wiped his mouth and pushed back his sweaty hair.

But I saw the mast. I know I did. I saw the sails. I saw the lines and rigging. He kicked the rocks to find it.

It must be buried, he reasoned, and, bracing himself against a boulder, avalanched the stones with his feet. They rolled, bounced and cracked into dust deep in the crater. Still he found no ship. Getting to his knees, he dug with his hands. Stone smoke burned his nose, and his eyes watered.

An hour passed. Finally Tomás rolled to his back and, disillusioned, looked up at the blue, blue sky for comfort.

A solitary frigatebird soared above him like a black cross. To Tomás the lonely symbol spoke of dark things to come.

What does it mean? he asked himself.

An hour later he slowly picked his way down the mountain.

The Reef Sends a Warning

AT the bottom of the volcano Tomás walked across the sunny plateau where Ramón and Miguel had spread out the salted fish to dry, and ran down the dyke to the beach.

Disillusioned and saddened by his discovery, he sat down in his father's chair, wondering how he would tell Miguel there was no ship. After thinking about it for a time, he decided he would not. The island had been so much more beautiful when the ship had been there. It had glowed with gold lights and had boomed with the sounds of winds filling sails and rattling ancient riggings. He would not spoil that for Miguel.

The matter settled, he ambled out onto the rock reef, which was now above water. The tide was almost all the way out, exposing the rocks like the spine of a lizard. They were uncovered at about the same hour each day, for the Sea of Cortez has a twelve-hour tide, not the twice-a-day ebb and flood that exists along most of the U.S. coasts. This is due to the movement of the water as it rocks in the Sea of Cortez, and the way the gulf lies in relation to the earth's axis and the moon.

On the last stone of the reef Tomás sat himself down in a busy world. Waves of little hermit crabs that had been left high and dry by the tide scurried on their pointed toes. Carrying the heavy shells in which they lived, they ran toward the scent of water. In the tidal pool at his feet the increasing light told the sea anemones the tide was almost out. They began closing their flowerlike tendrils to survive the long hours in stale water. The *hachas*, little oysters, were already closed for the duration, while over the top of the brown seaweed danced a lively ballet troupe of Sally Lightfoot crabs. In their brilliant red armor, they all skittered backward simultaneously when Tomás lifted his hand. They swept forward like a chorus line when he sat still.

Tomás took off his clothes and, picking up a heavy rock, jumped into the water. He was quickly plunged twelve feet down to the white coral sand at the bottom of the reef. Why there was white coral sand on a red-and-black volcanic island was a mystery that Tomás wondered about. He looked around for an answer each time he dived. Perhaps he would find an ancient white coral reef under the sea on one of his trips.

Tomás grinned as he beheld a world more fantastic than anything he could conjure up in his imagination. Blue, green, black, yellow, orange and purple fish floated dreamlike from the top of the reef to the bottom. On the rocks clung animals that looked like flowers, fans, strings, rubber tires, spaceships and Aztec gods. And they were all real.

Tomás frightened a pretty, four-inch damselfish. It swam away, gathered courage and returned to Tomás's face. Lifting its lancelike fins, it opened its mouth and challenged him to battle. Tomás was on its property, five square feet of algae-covered reef and the water several feet in front of it. The green-gray fish was a farmer. It grew and weeded an algae crop upon which it fed. Tomás knew this fish well. He plucked a piece of algae to say he had accepted the damselfish's challenge to fight. He had often seen rival damselfish do this and stir up a battle. It worked for Tomás, too. Instantly the little fish attacked, striking and biting him with its mouth. Tomás grinned mischievously and stopped teasing his courageous little friend.

An iridescent green-blue parrot fish came out of a cave and inspected Tomás. They also knew each other. Every time Tomás dived here this very same bumphead parrot fish greeted him by tipping on his side and contemplating him out of an eye encircled with long, lashlike streaks. Tomás blew a bubble, and the handsome fish snapped his bright-blue beak. It was composed of heavy tooth plates that audibly scraped algae from the rocks. Tomás would have followed the parrot fish to his cave had he not been running out of breath. Remembering the grebe, he decided to stay down longer, even though his lungs hurt. He began counting. At seven he dropped the rock and shot to the surface.

After taking many deep breaths, he picked up another rock and went down again. The sunlight bounced off the white seafloor and illuminated a garden of purple sea fans that stood among rippling ribbons of copper-colored seaweed. A school of three-banded butterfly fish swam overhead, circling like a wheel. Tomás looked up, through and around them into a kaleidoscope of light and color. Suspended in this beautiful water space, watching the fantastic in a world of fantastics, Tomás no longer cared that there was no ship.

Once more his lungs hurt. Determined to increase their capacity, he held on to the rock and sat resolutely on the bottom. Just in front of him lay an overhang. The sea currents that rushed along the reef here had eroded it, leaving the deep, dark overhang. Tomás swam a short distance under it, looking for his friend the jewfish, which lived in the cave at the bottom of the sea. The fish had large, black eyes that had evolved for night hunting, the time when the jewfish fed. When it did not appear, Tomás forced himself to hold his breath yet longer and swam farther under the overhang.

And then he saw something else. Far to his right loomed the tail of a huge shark. He could not see the head, for the beast was moving in and out of focus in the darkness of the cavern. But what he saw was big. It must be the whale shark that Miguel had seen swimming up from the deep water, ripping nets as it came.

Tomás still held his breath, determined to get a better look at his shark. The salt water was burning his eyes now, and all he could see was a tail vanishing into watery gloom. He dropped the rock and kicked up toward air.

As he rose he looked down. The shark cast a shadow as it moved along the whole course of the overhang, some one hundred feet. Tomás could not see the head or the yellow spots on the body that would tell him it was a whale shark; but he knew it was a shark. It was constantly moving. Sharks must keep swimming to stay alive. These fish, whose ancestors appeared in the seas 150 million years ago, cannot get oxygen unless they are streaming ahead. They have no air bladders and no gill covers to pump the aerated water over their gills. The shark is doomed to eternally swim forward to force water through its gill clefts. Because sharks must move, shark fishermen do not have to fight the dangerous fish. Their nets hold them still, and the sharks drown. They cannot swim backward.

Tomás surfaced, gasped air and grabbed another rock. He wanted to see the whole body of his whale shark. He plunged to the bottom again and peered under the overhang.

The shark had gone, swimming slowly but constantly forward. Dropping his rock, Tomás made a more leisurely ascent this trip and noticed that there was not one fish on the reef now. Their absence should have been a warning—fish flee when killer sharks are around—but he would not let the warning in. There was not a ship, but there *was* a whale shark.

Just before he surfaced, he saw a blurry body serpentine into the distance and disappear.

"It's him!" Tomás spluttered into the sunlight. "It's him!" Clambering up onto the reef, he grabbed his clothes and was dressing when the Evinrude 55 sounded beyond the tip of the cove and the Tórreses' boat came into view.

"Miguel! Grandpapa!" he called. Bouncing goatlike over the rocks, he headed for the beach to greet them.

Miguel drove the boat up onto the sand as far as it would go and jumped out.

"Any luck?" Tomás asked.

"One small hammerhead," Miguel answered, lifting a three-foot-long torpedo of silvery-gray flesh and cartilage from the boat.

"It's a great hammerhead," said Ramón. "A baby, but it will bring us a few extra pesos for Christmas."

Tomás carried the fish to the cleaning table, surprised that so small a shark could be so heavy. What would his huge whale shark weigh? He would, indeed, need Quetzalcoatl to help him lift it.

The great hammerhead Ramón and Miguel had caught was a youngster of the largest species of the hammerhead shark family, a family that consists of the hammerhead and the shovelhead sharks. They are man-eaters. On occasion, human remains have been found in the stomachs of all species.

Their weirdly designed heads have earned them their names, shaped as they are like hammerheads and shovels. No one knows why they are shaped this way. One guess is that the strange heads balance them in the water like the fins on an airplane's tail. Another is that the widely separated eyes give the fish binocular vision, the better to catch their prey. Their mouths are slung far under their heads, and because—like those of all sharks—both jaws move up and down, the jaws open fearsomely wide, making it easy to kill its victim.

Tomás lifted the top jaw of the baby hammerhead and looked at the rows and rows of formidable teeth. The front tier, which was a line of sharp triangles, stood upright. Six more rows lay prone behind it. These were replacements. Each row would move steadily forward to eventually replace the front row when it became dulled and was shed after seven or eight days of voracious feeding. Then a new row would take its place.

"Grandpapa," Tomás said when Ramón joined him at the cleaning table, "can I have these jaws to clean and sell?" Propped open and dried, the jaws were a favorite souvenir for the American tourists, and they paid well for them.

"You may have them," said Ramón, "provided you don't buy any more gunpowder for José's fireworks." Tomás threw back his head and laughed from his heart.

"I wouldn't do that," he said, "now, would I?" He smiled innocently.

Ramón harumphed.

"Clean them carefully," Ramón said, removing his fish knife from its sheath on his belt. "A shark has no bones, just cartilage. It's easily damaged; and if it is, you won't get a good price for it."

After sharpening his knife, Ramón cut the tough sharkskin from mouth to tail. Grabbing the head, he pulled off the skin with his plyers, moving swiftly and steadily so as not to damage it. Sharkskin was valuable.

"Grind some salt for me, Tomás," he said. "We'll prepare the shark tonight. Tomorrow we are going to bring in the nets and go home for the weekend. The Christmas festival has begun."

"You don't want to work tomorrow?" asked Miguel, who had joined them. "We have very few fish to sell."

"We might as well give up and enjoy ourselves," Ramón answered with a sigh. "The fishing is terrible." Tomás was startled. He had never heard his grandfather give up before. He looked at him. Ramón's mouth was drawn down and his black, deep-set eyes lacked their usual sparkle. Tomás worried to see him so discouraged. Ramón was the sun and the moon and the stars, everything constant and reliable. He must not change. Perhaps, Tomás thought, if I tell him about the whale shark, he will smile again. The three of us together can carry it into the plaza, holding it high above our heads.

Then he remembered the ship. Maybe there was no whale shark, either. He did not speak out.

"No *oficiales*?" Miguel asked Tomás.

"No *oficiales*," replied Tomás. They were myths too.

Griselda

THE following afternoon Miguel took the helm and steered the *ponga* homeward. As the boat skimmed past the rock reef, Tomás stood on the bow and looked down into the red-orange sea, which now reflected the colors of the sunset. He saw nothing larger than the parrot fish.

The *ponga* shot out of the cove and into the Shallows, which lay between the island and the peninsula. The water was only about fifteen feet deep. Many sharks came here to give birth to their live young or to lay eggs, as some do. Into these protected waters also came old and ill sharks. They could slow their continuous swimming by heading into the currents and letting the swiftly flowing water rush through their gills. They used less energy this way and could rest and heal themselves. And into these waters came the Torres men to maintain their reputation as Loreto's best shark fishermen. The Shallows were sometimes called the Torres.

In mid current Tomás raised his hand to signal Miguel to slow down the boat. He leaned far out and looked for his shark but saw only the sand sculptures on the bottom that had been carved by the currents, and a silver river of anchovies. They were spreading out and sinking as they prepared to sleep for the night.

"Okay," Tomás called to Miguel. "Go on." Hardly had he spoken than the anchovies flashed like a single warning light and were gone. The sea bottom was clear of fish, but Tomás had dropped to his seat and did not see this message from the anchovies.

Miguel speeded up the motor. The wind tugged at Tomás's Mexican Soccer Team cap, and he took it off, smiling as his hair whipped across his broad, brown forehead. There was no Spanish galleon, but somewhere around here there was a shark for him.

Five miles south of Coronados Island the village of Loreto came into view. Miguel took a fix on the mission bell tower and steered toward it. The low, red sun shone through its arched Byzantine windows, turning them into a fiery lighthouse. The mission bell tower had been a navigational guide for the seamen of Loreto since 1695. That year a mule that was carrying the statue of the Virgin for a new mission stopped in its tracks and refused to go on. Interpreting this as a message from God, Jesuit Father Juan Maria Salvatierra ordered the mission be built on the spot where the mule was standing. Since its completion, the mission has been transferred from the Jesuits to Franciscan monks, bombarded in battles with Baja Indians and then U.S. troops, cared for, neglected and, most recently, rebuilt.

Whether whole or standing in ruins, the bell tower guided the fishermen of Loreto home to their families.

A ray of light struck the glass windows in the dome and set off a sun flash. Tomás smiled. A sunburst was a very good omen no matter where you saw one, but particularly on the tower of the mission of Loreto.

That cancels the black cross, he said to himself, and looked forward to the weekend.

The wind, which had begun to rise around two P.M., as it does every afternoon on the Sea of Cortez, blew gradually stronger, until the *ponga* was buried between waves. Miguel steered up their steep slopes, sailed off their crests and crashed down into dark troughs. Spray flew ten feet high as they sped along the beach where Victorio, the sportfishing fleet captain, kept his twelve boats. Tomás counted them; they were all in. Victorio brought the gringos home at one P.M., before the winds arose.

In the prankish waves close to shore several of Tomás's classmates bobbed. They laughed and shouted as they rode to the tops of crests that sparkled with the reflected Christmas lights of houses along the beach. Among the swimmers was Griselda, the girl from Mexico City. Tomás called out and waved to her. She splashed water and waved back.

Griselda was like no other girl Tomás knew. She had come from a Mexico he did not know. Like no other girl, she waited for him at the Café Olé and walked to school with him, and like no other girl he knew, her parents were divorced, a word he had had to look up in the dictionary. She and her mother had moved to Loreto to live with Griselda's uncle Victorio and his wife, Bárbara. Griselda was quite beautiful but very unusual looking by Tomás's mestizo standards. Her skin was a creamy tan, her eyes were almost green and her hair, which fell to her shoulders in waves, was light brown. Griselda had inherited her lovely coloring from her Norwegian father. Although she smiled and looked happy in school, Tomás knew she was not. She sometimes cried as she walked with him to the junior high.

"I am homesick for Mexico City," she had told him one day when he had asked about her tears. "It is so busy and beautiful, with so much to do." He had tried to cheer her up that day by telling her about the Spanish galleon on the top of the volcano. She had laughed and looked at him doubtfully. A few days ago, when he had sensed her unhappiness, he had dared to tell her about his whale shark. She liked this story and had even clapped when he came to the part where he, Tomás, held the shark high and the mission bells rang.

"That's fun," she had said. "I would like to see that. A whale shark over your head would make Loreto bearable."

Griselda went out of Tomás's mind as the *ponga* sped past the Mission Hotel and the palm-leaf-covered trailer where Tía and Tío, two retired Americans, lived. They taught English to the children and adults of Loreto as a gift of thanks to the Mexicans for being so warm and hospitable. The boat dashed past the Siesta Inn, where the sportfishermen stayed, and a few small casas, then headed in to the commercial fishermen's beach. Miguel ran the *ponga* ashore. Tomás was home.

The three fishermen jumped out and smiled to a group of unemployed men who were idling away time on the beach. They gathered around to watch the Tórreses unload. Watching is a national pastime in Mexico, and only occasionally does someone step forward to help.

When the boat was unloaded, Ramón sought out a sharp-eyed man sitting under a palm tree, wearing a waist-length fur coat.

"Do you have time to pull us up, Zoro?" Ramón asked, although the man was obviously doing nothing.

Zoro—"the fox"—nodded and got to his feet. His skinny, bare legs stuck out from under the fur coat like lollipop sticks. He had fair skin that was deeply tanned and eyes as yellow as his namesake's. Zoro beckoned to a group of men with their hands in their pockets.

"Come," he said, and they shuffled forward, grabbed the sides of the *ponga* and, on a signal from Zoro, ran the boat swiftly up the beach to above the high-tide line. There it would sit until Monday morning, when the Tórreses would go to sea again. They would not need Zoro and his cronies for the launch. At five A.M. the tide would be lapping the stern of the *ponga,* and it was easily pushed into the water.

After thanking Zoro, Ramón lifted a large bundle of shark fins to his shoulder. Salted and dried, they were ready to be sold to the wholesaler.

"Did you see the *oficiales*?" Zoro asked him.

"Not a sign of them," Ramón answered.

"Strange," said Zoro. "It is rumored that they are here to speak to us commercial fishermen."

Ramón shifted his load. "What do you make of it?"

"Who knows?" answered Zoro. "*Oficiales* are crazy."

Tomás threw his bag of belongings over his shoulder and walked up the wide dirt street, leaving his grandfather and uncle discussing the peculiarities of government with Zoro.

Above him the branches of old mesquite and olive trees along the street bent and rustled as the winds of evening blew through them. Children laughed behind palm-leaf fences and ran in the street. Cocks crowed, dogs barked and pigs grunted. The sounds were comforting and reassuring to Tomás. He was home.

A firecracker went off.

"José," he said, and grinned. "He's done it again." His friend José was a dreamer too. But he did not dream about catching sharks; he dreamed about making gorgeous fireworks that would light up the sky above Loreto on every holiday, and especially on Christmas Eve.

Tomás stopped at the crossroads and looked across the wide arroyo that separated Colonia Zaragosa, the fishermen's district, from the busy center of Loreto. The dusty desert town had taken on an air of enchantment and fiesta. Christmas lights glittered in shop windows along the main street and on streetlamps and palm trees. Through the rosy, sunlit dust he could faintly make out the plaza, tree lined and spacious. The government workers who had been fitting small stones between the fluted bricks on the plaza were getting up off their hands and knees and packing away their tools. The day's work was over. They would collect their daily five thousand pesos and go home. Many would stop by the beer hall beforehand, and some of these, Tomás well knew, would not make it home until morning. This was the beginning of the two-week celebration of the birth of Jesus, a time for music, dancing, fireworks and breaking piñatas.

Tomás hurried toward his grandfather's casa, the third palm-leaf enclosure from the corner. The gate was open to greet the fishermen, and he ran in.

"Anyone home?" he called.

"Tomás!" A little girl with black, curly hair ran out of the nearest of three *palapas* and into his arms.

"María!" he said, swinging her around. "Why are you so excited?"

"I'm helping your mother," the five-year-old answered. "Francisca and I are putting beautiful red crepe paper around the picture of the Lady of Guadalupe. We are making an altar—a pretty Christmas altar. Come see it."

María pulled him down the earthen path to a palm-thatched roof that served as a foyer. Next to this was the kitchen, a *palapa* hung with pots and pans and open on two sides to the breeze and the light. Across from the foyer stood a three-walled room and beyond it two four-walled sleeping *palapas.* On one of these hung a white cloth on which a calendar painting of the Virgin of Guadalupe was mounted. She was encircled with crepe paper and cascades of cherry-red bougainvillea.

"It's beautiful, María," Tomás exclaimed, and squeezed her hand. Little María was a distant relative whose parents had died last year. When Digna, Miguel's wife, had learned about the orphan, she had gone to La Paz and brought her back to Ramón's casa. The happy little María helped to soothe Digna's grief over the loss of her own children, and she spoiled her as much as she did Tomás. To Tomás his little adopted sister was wonderful and funny, and he enjoyed her enormously.

He admired the altar once more, then walked out to behind the outhouse, where his mother was taking down the laundry. He greeted her warmly, but with restraint. He was fourteen now and talking politics with the men. This required a new dignity of him. Francisca sensed this and nodded respectfully.

"You are getting big," she said. "Every time you come back from the island, you are wider and taller." He laughed and she put an arm around him. Tomás felt her happiness spill over into him. He broke down and hugged her. Then he pushed away.

"The *oficiales* want to talk to us fishermen," he said authoritatively. Francisca frowned and picked up the basket of clothes. She, too, shared the national dread for the *oficiales.*

"What will they do?"

"Nobody knows. We'll have to wait and see."

Francisca smiled at Tomás's forbearance. He was usually an impatient child. How proud his father would be to see his son coming of age. She still grieved for his father and for herself. Without him she was just another pair of hands doing what had to be done. With him she had been a woman of importance.

"We'll have to wait and see," Tomás repeated, and walked off to the three-sided *palapa* where he slept.

The baby bed that had held Tomás, his cousins and now María stood on one side of the room. Behind it was a chest of drawers. On a wooden rod slung between the beams hung the family's wardrobe, perhaps two or three outfits for each person, most well worn. Shoes, hats and boxes were lined up neatly on the strut below the roof.

Tomás sat down on his bed, a hand-woven pad on the floor. Near his pillow sat a box. He opened it and took out a steel spearhead and a whetstone, both of which had belonged to his father. He began sharpening the spearhead. When it was too dark to see, he joined his grandmother, Dolores, in the kitchen. She was flattening balls of corn dough into perfect circles with her tortilla press. Cactus fruit and yellowtail fish fillets dipped in cornmeal were frying in a pan that sat on legs above a small fire on the sandbox stove. There was no electricity in the Tórreses' casa. "It's very dangerous," Ramón had said. "It killed a friend of mine, charred him like a chicken thrown into the hot coals. I will never have electricity in my house."

Nobody missed it. The family went to bed and got up with the sun, and water was provided by the town pump. It came into the casa through a long, green hose. The one radio, which belonged to Miguel, ran on batteries.

"Smells good," Tomás said to his grandmother, a slender woman with dark eyes and a finely shaped nose reminiscent of the nose of a woman in one of the old Spanish paintings in the mission. Dolores was not far from her Spanish ancestors. As the head of Ramón's household she was greatly respected by Francisca and Digna. Ramón and Miguel adored her, as did Tomás. But his love for her was not the same as his love for his mother. She came first.

Tomás leaned close, to watch his grandmother work. She brushed him away.

"Dinner will soon be ready," she said. "Go fetch Ramón and Miguel. They must still be at the fish buyer's casa."

Hardly had she spoken when Ramón and Miguel opened the gate and stepped inside talking seriously. Dolores and Digna hurried to greet them. The gate clicked shut. The Tórreses were all home, safely gathered within the walls of their land. Here in the cozy shadows, lit only by the flickering light of the cooking fire, they all felt safe—safe from worldly troubles—the *oficiales*, the dwindling fish supply and the wholesaler who, once again, had not paid the going rate for the shark fins. The next buyer, he knew, was a hundred miles away in La Paz.

Ramón and Miguel pulled the water hose under the pomegranate tree and showered themselves while also watering the plant. Water is precious in the desert.

"What's for dinner?" Miguel asked as he sat down at the long blue table.

"Napolitos and fish," answered Dolores. "And a surprise. Peppers stuffed with shrimp."

"My favorite," said Tomás, plunking himself down in his chair.

When the main courses were finished, Digna, who was in charge of desserts, passed around her dates stuffed with sugar and nuts; then she sat down close to Miguel and smiled up at him. Digna had a wide, flat face with round, rosy cheeks. Her curly hair was quite beautiful, but Tomás had little time for her. She talked only about María and Miguel and the children she was going to have someday. She even had names for them.

"She dreams, too," Tomás said of her one day, "but not of great things like ships and sharks."

Digna lit a candle when the cook fire died down. In the soft light the Torres men drank their coffee and discussed the Japanese factory boats. The wholesaler had gone aboard one in La Paz, and what he had seen astonished Ramón and Miguel. It was, he had said, a city, with stores and storerooms, offices, and equipment for processing fish, and things that even the wholesaler did not understand. The women were quiet during the discussion. Presently María climbed into her bed and softly sang herself to sleep.

When the coffee cups were empty, Digna wiped them clean and followed Miguel to their bedroom *palapa.* Ramón and Dolores held hands in the darkness for a little while, listening to the low, trilling call of the lesser nighthawks. When the owls called, they too went off to bed.

Francisca was still up, kneeling in prayer before the Lady of Guadalupe. Presently she went off to her sleeping mat in the *palapa* with Tomás and María.

Tomás was in bed but not asleep. He had pulled his blanket over his head and was reading by flashlight a book on sharks that Juan Fuertes had lent him.

"Whale sharks are sluggish," he read, then thought about the shark of the reef. My shark fits that description perfectly, he thought, and clicked off his light, smiling to himself.

From across the arroyo came the music of the mariachi band at the Loreto Cabaret. The first song of the all-night, fourteen-day celebration rang out. Tomás was glad he had a shark to think about, for it was going to be a long, sleepless night. The two-week-long Christmas festival was in full swing.

Ships and Sharks and Factory Boats

AT home Tomás's alarm clock was Gallo, the fighting cock that lived next door. His crowing, like that of all the cocks of Loreto, sounded like *enchilada,* not *cock-a-doodle-doo.* Tomás awakened and looked up at the mosaic of palm leaves on the ceiling and waited for the next alarm to go off. Presently he heard it: the *dingdong, dingdong* of the mission bells. To the fishermen of Colonia Zaragosa this early call to Mass was their call to the water. Tomás did not move. More alarms were to come.

The dogs barked next. First Papo, who lived across the street, then Bruja, a homeless dog who made a living along the main road to Loreto. From the other side of the arroyo Osado, the bank manager's dog, tuned in with a sharp retort. Then all the dogs greeted the day. Their concert was followed by silence. Tomás waited. One more voice was to be heard. At last it came—seven high yips. Macho, José's dog, was speaking. Tomás got up.

Dolores had already lit the mesquite twigs on the sand table. The light from the flames danced over the walls and ceiling of the *palapa* like windblown quetzal feathers.

"Grandmama," Tomás said, "I'm going to take our little *ponga* and go to the island today."

"You cannot at this moment," she answered, dipping her hand into the cornmeal canister. "Miguel has already taken it to Carmen Island to get salt at the salt mine." Tomás frowned and thought for a moment.

"Then I will catch a ride with Zoro. He works on Saturday and Sunday." Dolores made no comment. She picked up a piece of salt fish that had been soaking in water overnight and placed it in a frying pan. To Tomás her silence seemed to ask for an explanation.

"I will spear you a sea bass," he said avoiding the real reason. "I'm almost as good as my father at spearing fish." Dolores still did not say anything. She did not disapprove of Tomás's plans; she just no longer felt it proper to tell Tomás what he could and could not do. He was fourteen.

"I'm off," he announced. "Tell Grandpapa I've gone to the island."

"I'll tell him when he awakens. It may be noon," she said. "He did not sleep well last night. His legs are bothering him again. It's the circulation, the nurse at the infirmary told him."

Reference to ailments and sickness were not to Tomás's liking. He would rather not hear about them. Hastily he pocketed a leftover stuffed pepper and kissed his grandmother good-bye.

The cardinal whose mate had built a nest in the edible bean tree sang his *pretty bird* song to her as Tomás walked out the gate. Papo barked and crossed the street, to join Tomás as he ran past José's casa. Halfway along, the sound of an outboard motor sent Tomás's feet flying. He arrived at the water's edge, only to see Zoro well on his way to sea. No one else was around. Tomás sat cross-legged on an overturned boat and thought about what to do next. Griselda came to mind. He would ask her to get him a ride to the island in one of Victorio's sportfishing boats. Tomás started up the road, with Papo at his heels wagging his tail in the joy of being in Tomás's presence.

On his return he again passed José's house without stopping to ask if it had been he who had set off the tremendous firecracker last night. It had to be, and he was in a hurry. At the edge of the arroyo Papo ran into Bruja, the yellowish dog with the wiry muzzle who owned the territory along the road. Both dogs rushed at each other and sniffed noses and tails while circling with bristling ruffs and exposed canine teeth. Tomás left Papo working out the politics of just who was boss dog.

In the middle of the arroyo Tomás stopped. He glanced up the dry riverbed to the distant trees and remembered that he needed a shaft for his spearhead. The trees were straighter on the arroyo bank than on the island, and he headed out to find one. Picking his route carefully in the semidarkness, he made his way toward the mountains. He knew the arroyo well. He and José caught rattlesnakes here, and although it was too cool for them to be out this morning, he avoided their lairs. He also knew the arroyo chipmunks. Raya, who lived under the twisted mesquite log, would eat out of his hand when he called him. Tomás squeaked, but Raya did not appear. It had been cold enough for a blanket last night. Raya would still be underground in his warm, grassy nest. Tomás put a mesquite bean by his door and went on.

On the top of a clump of organ-pipe cactus sat a magnificent caracara, the two-foot-high falcon that is the national emblem of Mexico. He was flapping his wings, preparing them for flight. His long legs and bare, red face were barely visible in the low light, but Tomás could see his white neck well. It shone like a pearl necklace below his black cap and above his black-and-brown body. The caracara cackled harshly. Tomás saluted him.

As he hurried along, the plants told him he was leaving the coast and heading toward the mountains. The morning glory vines and pencillike ocotillo became more abundant, and the horizon was not just stippled but forested with the giant cardón cactus. Most of these telephone poles of chlorophyll and spines stood forty feet tall. Tomás did no more than glance at them. He was searching for hardwood trees, not cacti, particularly for green, leafy trees. A two-year drought had forced the trees to drop their leaves to prevent precious water from evaporating from their surfaces. As they bent toward the slightest moisture, the trees had twisted. Tomás wanted a straight tree, and he knew where to find one. Most of the water that rushed through the arroyo after the winter and summer cloudbursts drained into the sea; but some of it sank into the ground and was held in subterranean reservoirs of pebbles and sand. Over these spots the elephant and jatropha trees were green, and the *palo blanco* grew straight.

When Tomás saw the control tower at the Loreto airport, he climbed the bank, walked into a grove of trees with feathery green leaves and looked around. Several stalks were possibilities, but one *palo blanco* was perfect. With his knife he cut off five feet of it and returned to the road to Loreto.

Bruja joined him, his ear bleeding from the encounter but apparently the victor. Papo was not to be seen. Bruja took up the position at Tomás's heels and trotted along in the dust. Having once been fed half a burrito by Tomás, he never forgot this dear friend and joined him whenever he had the opportunity.

Loreto was waking as they came into town. Señora Madero was sweeping the grassless clay outside her *palapa,* and her son was in the street, watering the dirt road to keep down the dust that would soon be stirred up by the traffic.

The stores would not open until ten. They would close at noon, reopen at four o'clock and stay open until the restaurants and bars closed in the small hours of the morning.

Tomás stopped before the window of Stereolandia, a store that to him was a glimpse of the United States. The shelves and floor were stacked with radios, television sets, cassette players, washing machines, dishwashers, computers and kitchen devices. They were as unobtainable as spaceships.

Next door was a *palapa* with clay floors, boxes, tires, and clothes hanging from lines and poles. Tomás looked from one to the other. Stereolandia was the United States, the *palapa* was his Mexico.

How can two neighbors who lie side by side on the same continent be so very, very different? Tomás asked himself as he looked in the window of Stereolandia.

He walked on to the plaza. The mission rose strong, massive and beautiful on one side; steps and an unfinished fountain lay on the other. He paused to decide where he would stand to hold up his shark—before the great wooden mission door? Under the bell tower? Right out in the middle of the plaza? He did not have time to make up his mind. The huge shark that lurked under the overhang of the rock reef would not wait forever for him. He jogged on.

As he came out onto the seaside road, he saw that it was later than he thought. The pickup trucks were grinding along the shore road, bringing the gringo fishermen from the inns and hotels to Victorio's. He broke into a run.

At Victorio's high-walled hacienda and fishing camp, he peered in the gate to see if Griselda was about. In the center of the earthen yard sat a large brick casa surrounded by elegant *palapas* that were not of mestizo design. They were large and square, with steeplelike roofs. The palm thatch was clipped neatly, like a new haircut. Tomás thought they must have been designed in Hollywood, the U.S. town most talked about in Loreto.

Victorio kept his land well. The yard had been freshly swept and raked. Gardens of bright red and yellow flowers were edged with the bones of great whales. Every March the blue whales and gray whales came to the Sea of Cortez. Old ones died or were killed, and their bones would wash up on Baja's rocky coast. Against the dark shore they loomed like great white tombstones, and the fishermen reverently gathered them to decorate their casas and gardens.

Griselda was not to be seen, and Tomás went on to the sportfishermen's beach, not quite certain what he was going to do. He did not think he had the courage to ask Victorio for a ride. Victorio was a very important man, not only in Loreto but in Mexico City. He was rich and had political connections in high places in the government.

The sun was glowing below the rim of the sea when Tomás arrived at the beach. The morning star was as bright as a headlight. Tomás sat down on an overturned boat and watched Victorio equip the gringos with rods and reels and assign them guides and boats. Perhaps one of the guides would be from Colonia Zaragosa and Tomás would not be embarrassed to ask him for a ride to the island. One by one the boats were shoved into the water, and one by one they rode out into the sunrise, captained by strange guides from fishing towns north of Loreto. Tomás whittled the tip of his pole shaft to fit into his spearhead and waited.

As the last boat was launched, Tomás despaired. He did not know that guide either. But wait! Who was that! He jumped to his feet. One of the people shoving the *ponga* into the water was Griselda. He could not believe his eyes—a girl doing a man's work! He turned his back so as not to embarrass her. She probably would not want one of her friends to see her launching a boat. Griselda turned around.

"Tomás!" she called, and came running to meet him, no more embarrassed by what she had been doing than if she had been sewing robes for the padre.

"It's nice to see you," she said, rolling down her sleeves. "I've never seen you on this side of town before. What are you doing here?"

For a moment he could not remember just why he was there, he was so stunned by the sight of her launching a boat. She even looked like a water person. Her hair was tied back from her face with a ribbon, and she wore blue jeans. A loose white blouse completed her outfit. He finally thought of something to say.

"I was wondering if anyone knows what the *oficiales* want of the commercial fishermen."

"Probably to tell them the good news," Griselda promptly answered.

"The good news?"

"Yes. The government has stopped the Japanese factory boats from fishing the Sea of Cortez."

"Really?" Tomás exclaimed. "Is that true?" It had never occurred to him that the *oficiales* could be bearers of good news. "The Japanese are gone? You are sure?"

"Oh, yes. Uncle Victorio and Aunt Bárbara told me. They have been going to Mexico City every month for almost a year to ask the Minister of Fisheries to keep the factory boats out of the Sea of Cortez. They kept telling him they were ruining the fishing and that the Mexicans are suffering. Last night the Minister's secretary telephoned Victorio. She said the Minister had stopped the factory boats from fishing here. Good news, isn't it?"

Tomás was amazed. He found it hard to believe that a Loreto fisherman, even one as rich as Victorio, could speak to someone in the government and that the Minister of Fisheries had listened to him and done what he'd asked. This was more fantastic than the window at Stereolandia.

"If you don't believe me," Griselda said, "come to the hacienda with me. It'll probably be announced on the morning TV news." She pulled his sleeve, and they started off.

"Thank you," he said when they arrived at Victorio's, "but I had better go home. The news will make my family very happy."

Griselda started to go in the gate, then turned back.

"Have you told Señor Fuertes what you are going to do next year?"

Tomás was so overwhelmed with the good news that for a moment he did not know what she was talking about.

"You mean about going to high school?" he said, recovering.

"Yes, of course. It's important."

"I haven't done anything about it," Tomás said. "I am not sure what I'll do."

"Go to school, Tomás. You are very smart," Griselda said. "It's the only way to get out of this pit and live a pleasant life."

"What pit?" Tomás asked.

"This town," Griselda said, gesturing.

"This town?" He was amazed. "It's nice."

Griselda shrugged and, shaking her head, walked through the gate. Tomás stood where he was as she crossed the yard and went into the grand brick casa. Through the open door he could see a luxurious living room with upholstered chairs and broad couches. The casa must also have bathrooms, and an electric stove and washing machine like those in Stereolandia. Victorio's house was U.S. style—similar to the elaborate brick-and-tile mansions on "Gringo Street." These houses were so far from Tomás's world that he did not even want them. His dreams were of ships and sharks, and of factory boats leaving the Sea of Cortez.

"A joy has happened," he said, and ran all the way home.

The Whizbang Flare

TOMÁS was so full of good news that he was inside the casa gate before he recalled Griselda's remark about Loreto. What did she mean? The glossy leaves of the lemon tree sparkled in the sun, and the ripening pomegranates glowed like red Christmas balls. How could anyone possibly call Loreto a pit?

Ramón was up and apparently feeling better, for he was watering the banana tree that stood beside the kitchen *palapa.*

"Grandpapa! Grandpapa!" he shouted. "The Japanese fishing boats have been sent home."

Ramón turned around so quickly, the hose fell from his hand. The water splashed his bare feet and shot out over the ground.

"Is that true?"

"Yes, yes. Victorio's niece told me," Tomás answered. "There will be more fish in the sea!" He picked up the hose and handed it back to Ramón. "More fish in the sea. Everything is all right."

His mother heard and turned away from the wooden rack that hung down between two beams of the *palapa* porch. She had just laid a portion of beef from the *supermercado* upon it to dry in the desert air.

"Can this be true?" she asked Ramón.

"I don't know," Ramón said, turning off the water.

"It is," Tomás insisted. "The secretary of the Minister of Fisheries called Victorio last night and told him. Ask Miguel. I'll bet he knows."

"Miguel has not come back from Carmen Island," Ramón said. "Let's go to the beach. The fishermen ought to know." Ramón took a clean shirt from the pole and, after brushing his hair, tilted his straw hat over one eye with a flair and strode out of the gate with Tomás. Papo, who was sleeping under the olive tree across the street, got to his feet and shuffled along behind. A chicken flew up before them all, squawking.

No sooner had they crossed the road to Loreto than Tomás knew the good news was true. Women were talking excitedly across fences, fishermen were running toward the beach, shouting and asking questions. Dogs barked. Then a package of one-inch firecrackers went off, and another, and three more.

"That does it," said Tomás, raising both fists in the air and shaking them. "It is true!"

"Tomás!" José hand vaulted over his casa gate and caught up with him. "Tomás, the Japanese factory boats are gone. My father heard it from Victorio. I have a huge flare firecracker—a whizbang. Let's set it off."

"Where did you get it?"

"I made it, what else?"

"You made a whizbang?" Tomás asked incredulously. "I know you can make firecrackers, but when did you learn to make whizbangs?"

"Uncle López was here. You know my Uncle López, who works in the fireworks factory on the mainland? Well, he came to visit while you were on the island. He brought a lot of gunpowder and combustibles and showed me how to make a firecracker flare.

"And guess what? He left me the instructions and the material for making a huge rocket, one of those Roman candles. It will light up the sky of Loreto."

"I can see it already," said Tomás, looking up and shading his eyes with his hand. "It is roaring. It has turned red. Now it is bursting into feathers—they are the tail of a quetzal bird. It's gorgeous."

"Come on, Tomás." José was laughing with pleasure at Tomás's description. "Quit talking and help me set off the whizbang." Tomás saw that Ramón was already at the beach, talking to a group of men, and he followed José to his casa. Papo lay down in front of the gate and put his head on his paws. A cock strutted past his nose. Papo lunged; the bird squawked and flew into an olive tree. Both seemed very satisfied with themselves.

José and Tomás ran past a pile of refuse, a disassembled outboard motor, some gasoline cans, a gutted couch and three fighting cocks in cages and came to a halt before a stack of bricks. The Morélloses were building a new house, a brick house like Victorio's. They had been working on it off and on for three years, and it was far from finished and might never be. In the meantime Tomás and José had put the loose bricks to use, stacking them into a cavelike shelter with three walls that they roofed with a sheet of plywood. Here they had privacy. Inside, on a shelf, José's firecrackers and combustibles were stored in empty refried-bean cans and mole jars. Tomás kept his starfish, sea worms and echinoderms in shoe boxes beneath them. Tomás and José also kept their *Aguila* comic books stacked in a corner to read when they were able to sneak out of Sunday school or when they were bored.

José opened one of the new jars of combustibles his uncle had given him.

"This is for the rocket. I combine it with paper, gunpowder and fuses, and—zow!—it booms up over the mission bell tower."

"Will it have quetzal birds popping out of white eggs like you always dream about?"

"Not the first one. I will go slowly. The first one will explode into a red-and-yellow sunburst."

"Is it hard to do, José?" Tomás asked.

"Not when you know how. You just have to be careful."

"Real careful," added Tomás. "Gunpowder and combustibles are dangerous."

"Yes; they are," José said very seriously. "This stuff could blow a six-foot crater in our yard and take the pig and all of Papa's fighting cocks along with it.

"But I know what I'm doing," he added, and, with great confidence, reached into a refried-bean can and took out a lumpy firecracker.

"This is the whizbang flare," he said.

"Are we going to set it off now?" Tomás asked excitedly.

"No. We'll set it off tonight, in the dark, when everyone is celebrating. It's going to make the Day of No More Factory Boats a day to remember. The whizbang will be loud and bright." He closed his eyes and kissed the air. "Even the people in the United States will know that the factory boats are gone."

José's father was also a fisherman. Emiliano Morellos and his brother fished the Sea of Cortez for yellowtails, groupers and other fine eating fish. They used gill nets with a much smaller mesh than the nets of the shark fishermen—nets that Ramón disapproved of because they caught baby fish. To make a little extra money, the Morellos brothers also took an occasional gringo sportfisherman out for marlin, swordfish and tuna.

José carefully put the whizbang under his shirt and crawled out of the cave on his hands and knees. Tomás followed.

"Pick up some dates for the pig," José said. "We want to fatten her. We are going to butcher her for Christmas." Tomás gathered a handful of the dates that had fallen to the ground and tossed them to the large black-and-white sow that was tied to a palm tree by a rope. The sow rumbled to her feet and gulped them down with great satisfaction.

"She's good and fat," observed Tomás.

"Yummm," said José, and led Tomás through the kitchen to the tiled patio. José's mother, his Aunt Teresa and two of his six sisters were hanging out clothes on a line that stretched from the house to the fish icebox. José's father did not salt his fish. He chilled them on ice he bought at the Loreto icehouse and sold them fresh to the restaurants in town.

"Hello, Tomás," said José's pretty, round-faced mother. "How does Ramón like the good news?" Black-eyed Elena, José's youngest sister, smiled shyly at Tomás and ducked behind her mother's skirt.

"He's real happy, Señora Morellos," Tomás replied respectfully. "But he doesn't quite believe it. He's down at the beach, checking it out."

"It's true, all right," she said, then noticed José's bulging shirt. "What are you up to, José?"

"Tomás and I are going down to the beach to discuss politics," he answered with a mock frown.

"Get on with you," she said, shaking a wet shirt at him. The little girls giggled, and Aunt Teresa playfully snapped a towel at his ribs. José grabbed his stomach and rolled to the ground.

"Got me!" he cried, flopping to his back, pretending to be dead. "Tell Uncle Díaz I leave my cave to him." The girls were about to pounce on him when he jumped to his feet, and he and Tomás ran from the scene.

The beach was crowded. Almost every man in Colonia Zaragosa was either huddled in talk, drinking toasts to the Minister of Fisheries or laughing. No one was asleep under the palm trees. Tomás saw Ramón and Miguel at the water's edge, and he and José joined them near their little *ponga*. They all stared quietly out at the blue-violet Sea of Cortez, searching suspiciously for factory boats.

"Do you really suppose it's true?" Miguel asked Ramón.

"Don't you believe it, Miguel?" Tomás asked curiously.

"*Oficiales* say one thing and do something else," he said as Zoro and his son, Jesús, joined them.

"Yah, it's only a rumor," Zoro said. "No one has heard it announced on the television. It's just talk to hush up Victorio. He's been riding the minister hard."

"But it is true, Papa," said Jesús. "I heard it on the radio." Jesús was a large young man with a thick, round chest and very dark skin. He was as unlike his father in appearance as a fox is unlike a toad.

"Olé!" shouted a nearby fisherman who was plugged into a Walkman. "It is true! The newscaster just said so!" That seemed to make it final. Cassettes were turned up all over the beach. A young man plucked his guitar, and Colonia Zaragosa began what was to be an all-night fiesta to celebrate the departure of the Japanese factory boats—whether they wholly believed it or not.

At noon some enterprising families brought pushcarts to the beach and sold hot burritos, tamales, chimichangas and soda pop to the celebrants. Presently wives with children and babies arrived and clustered together under the palms in lively groups.

Miguel brought Dolores, Francisca, Digna and María to the beach and settled them on blankets and mats with José's mother and aunt and the little girls. Tomás and José went off to play soccer with their friends on the arroyo flood plain.

They came back from time to time to feast on Dolores's yellowtail enchiladas dipped in guacamole and on Señora Morellos's burritos. Music vied with hearty voices and loud laughter. The squeals of children running in and out of the crowd sounded like birdcalls above the lively din. By late afternoon the fiesta in Colonia Zaragosa was in full swing.

Tomás knew by the numbers of gulls that the party was a success. They circled over the beach in flapping crowds dropping down among the people, snatching food and fighting with each other over the bits and pieces. Their wings added a nimble zest to the fiesta.

As evening approached, Tomás and José edged down to the water's edge and sat on a log to wait and watch. Around five o'clock several hundred vultures circled high above the beach, then glided in low like a squadron of air-force jets coming home. When the sun sat on the top of the mountains, the vultures dropped into the palm trees to roost for the night. Shoving and squabbling, they secured their space and places, and the sun set swiftly and suddenly, as it does this close to the equator.

"Okay," said José, looking at the vultures. "The big birds are down."

"Darkness is ten minutes away," Tomás said.

With that they waded out to a large rock exposed by the ebb tide. No one took any notice of them. José propped up the lumpy whizbang with a shell, struck a match and held the flame against the fuse. Sparks sputtered. The fire burned toward the base of the flare. The boys ran.

"Kerboom!" A thunderous explosion was followed by a billowing cascade of red fire and smoke. A fountain of light shot up into the night, like flames from a dragon's mouth. Everyone stopped talking. The spectacle was accompanied by a wild mix of cassette music. José stood in the water, looking at the faces of the people now bright red in the hissing light. Their expressions of astonishment were worth all the study and work. He grinned broadly.

Then it was over. The flame went out.

"Olé!" called a fisherman.

"Who put that one off?" a woman asked.

"José Morellos," Tomás shouted. "And he made it himself!"

"Made it?" A group of boys crowded around José. The captain of the high-school soccer team and his friend lifted him to their shoulders and paraded him through the cheering crowd, which was calling and begging for another whizbang.

Tomás watched José revel in this moment of triumph. When he was lost from sight and the whoops had died down, Tomás waded out into the water and looked north. Coronados Island loomed black and still against the star-studded sky. He could almost see his shark.

Under the Overhang

THE fiesta for the Day of No More Factory Boats merged with the Christmas fiesta, and no one in Colonia Zaragosa or, for that matter, any of Loreto got much sleep. All Saturday and Sunday night mariachi bands played and families feasted and visited, and children romped until they fell down with sleep.

On Monday morning Gallo the cock announced the dawn only ten minutes after the last cassette player had been turned off. Tomás opened his eyes and looked up at the ceiling. It had been a grand party, and there was more to come.

"This feels like my day," he said, reaching for his spear, which was now mounted with the sharpened spearhead. He inspected its point. When the bells began ringing, Tomás got up without waiting for the dogs' alarm. He put on the clean trousers and shirt his mother had folded neatly beside his bed the night before and took out his whetstone. He began honing the spearhead to razor sharpness. The fresh scent of sunshine and homemade soap wafting up from his clothing made him think about Griselda's advice to get out of Loreto. He wondered how clean clothes would smell in another town, another state, another country. Would they smell of sunshine? Probably not.

María slumbered on, but Francisca got up in the dark and sleepily went off to the kitchen to dress in privacy. She picked up a broom and came back to begin her day's chores with the sweeping of the *palapas* and patio. She was always working, Tomás realized. Yesterday she had stayed home from one of the best beach parties simply to rake and burn the fallen leaves in the yard. As he thought about her, he realized that she rarely went anywhere except to gather wild foods and firewood and to visit the store and attend church. She was a mestizo woman through and through. Tomás had never heard her voice an opinion about politics; nor did she vote, although women had gained equal rights the year she was born. Once, when Tomás asked her why she did not, she told him she saw no purpose in voting. The president of Mexico was elected for a six-year term, and before he left office, he named his own successor. Everyone knew who the new president was going to be months before they went to the polls. "Why bother?" she had said.

Tomás could see her point; furthermore, there was also only one party to vote for—the "government party," called the Institutional Revolutionary Party, better known as the PRI. When Tomás had asked his social-studies teacher what happened to the opposition parties that emerged at election time, he had replied: The government has the means to ensure that they do not threaten its monopoly. Opposition leaders are either given influential jobs in the government or are quieted with money. All Mexicans know this, but they shrug and go on believing in their president. Only after the presidents leave office—and very often Mexico—with billions of government pesos do the people, too late, see them for what they are—modern-day Tezcatlipocas. To find the modern-day Quetzalcoatls, the mestizos looked to their families and the Lady of Guadalupe.

Tomás did not really think his mother stayed away from the polls because she thought it was useless to vote. He thought she stayed away because she did not think it was ladylike to be seen at the voting place. She considered herself a good woman—she gave birth, swept, cooked, washed, shopped, went to church and did not discuss politics. What, Tomás pondered, would his mother think of Griselda, who not only talked politics but launched boats and went fishing?

As he thought about his shy, hardworking mother, he wondered if she would even come to the plaza when he held his shark high over his head. Probably not; then he would have to carry his prize to her—down the main street, across the arroyo and up to the casa gate. He would put a wreath of flowers around her neck and bring her to the plaza with him. He loved his mother very much.

Having thought about these matters, he decided that being fourteen was great. He was pleased with his new awareness. But it meant also that he had to make up his mind. That was not so pleasant.

Rotating the spear, judging the sharpness of the point, he dared once again to think about his father. As always, these thoughts were fleeting and mystical—a vision of a shark, a skeleton of death and family stories about a man who was a great shark spearman as well as an intelligent, loving person. Tomás sometimes mixed him up with Quetzalcoatl.

Tomás shook his head and came back to the present. His grandfather was sitting at the blue table in the darkness. He seemed to be waiting for him. Perhaps he wanted to know what he was going to do with the spear. Tomás picked up his bundle of clothes and walked out to meet him.

Papo barked. Bruja answered. Tomás joined his grandfather.

"Would you carry my tackle box, Tomás?" he asked softly, so as not to be overheard by Dolores. "My leg is bothering me this morning." He glanced toward the kitchen *palapa,* where Dolores was working. "It doesn't hurt much, you understand, but I need a little help." Osado howled. His alarm was followed by the chorus of dogs. Macho gave seven high yips. Tomás smiled, took the tackle box and followed Ramón to the gate, where Miguel was talking softly to Digna and waiting for them.

No sooner were they on the road than Ramón and Miguel began chatting with their usual animation. This morning the talk was about inflation. Tomás listened. It seemed that inflation meant paying more and more pesos for fewer and fewer goods.

As they passed the Morellos's casa, Tomás looked over the palm wall to see if José was up. Macho ran up to the gate, yipping and barking. José was not to be seen, and Tomás presumed he was either sleeping or working on his Roman candle. José rarely went fishing with his father. Emiliano Morellos did not take him out because he wanted José to go to high school and learn English. Loreto, with its ancient missions, its beautiful waters, its delightful climate, was rapidly becoming a tourist town for Americans. Emiliano had noticed that kids who spoke English were getting good jobs. They worked for the bank, the luxurious government hotel El Presidente and the government travel bureau. What with the fishing getting worse and worse, Emiliano did not want his only son to follow in his footsteps. Consequently, José stayed home and was free to make firecrackers and read the thick book on pyrotechnics that Juan Fuertes, the science teacher, had lent him last year. After yesterday's triumph Tomás thought Emiliano was right. José should go to school, but not necessarily to learn English.

José's future brought up his own again. He still had not made up his mind what to do. He really did not know, and no one in the family but Miguel had voiced any opinion. It was as if Ramón and Tomás's mother, aunt and grandmother were waiting for the Virgin of Guadalupe to appear on the road and tell Tomás what he should do.

At the beach a slender, rather tall man was sitting against a date palm. As the Tórreses approached, he lifted his head from his knees and smiled.

"Good morning, Uncle Díaz," Tomás said. He knew the man well. He was José's uncle. As always, he was dressed in a white shirt with a collar and blue rayon trousers. He was very neat and clean despite having slept under the palm tree all night.

"Who is it?" Uncle Díaz asked, getting unsteadily to his feet.

"Me, Tomás Torres."

"Yes, yes. Good morning, Tomás," he said, leaning far to the left as he balanced himself like a gyroscope on some mystical spot. He lost his balance, took a quick step and, being unable to recover, gracefully circled the tree and came back. He grinned mischievously. Uncle Díaz was a handsome man with clean, chiseled features and curly, black hair that was grooved by his fingers' constantly running through it. His skin was dark, his cheeks a warm brick red and his teeth large and very white. They shone when he smiled.

"I am glad to see you," Uncle Díaz said, reaching out to touch Tomás's face. Tomás was pleased to hear this, for Uncle Díaz was his living hero. He had once been the most famous coral diver in Baja. Every day he had ridden out to the deeps between Carmen Island and Loreto, grabbed a rock from a supply on his boat, jumped overboard and gone down ninety feet. There in the dim gloom on the floor of the Sea of Cortez he had harvested the exquisite and very valuable black coral. After picking the coral, he would drop his rock and return to the surface, roaring as he emerged, gasping for air. He would hang on to the boat, breathing harshly until he had caught his breath. When his lungs had stopped aching, he would take another rock and plunge to the bottom again. Uncle Díaz, it was said, could stay down two whole minutes! How Tomás admired him.

After seven years the famous diver's career had ended. One day the *oficiales* banned the harvesting of black coral; it was almost extinct. Uncle Díaz was out of work. His ears had been injured by the terrible pressure at ninety feet, and his eyes had been burned by the sea salt. Unable to see or hear well enough to qualify for a government job, he had swept the patio and raked the yard of a wealthy gringo. While on this job he had discovered that tequila could bring back the beauty of the reefs and silence his ringing ears. He drank until he was fired.

Almost blind and nearly deaf, he walked up and down the shore road and main street looking for work. Finally his wife took their children and went home to live with her parents in La Paz. Uncle Díaz moved in with his brother Emiliano and his family. He was no trouble, José said. "He just drinks tequila and dreams away the days and nights. He's very sweet."

Tomás knew what alcohol did to many men. He had seen drunken fights in the street. He had heard children cry for help in the night when their fathers came home angry with alcohol madness. But Uncle Díaz was different. When the tequila stirred him, he told stories about the wonders under the sea. Tomás and José and his sisters would gather around him and listen. He told of the enormous, beautiful blue whales that he had touched and even kissed and of their kind, humanlike eyes. Sometimes he would tell about his two porpoise friends that had carried him to the surface when he had passed out at a great depth. He had tales to tell of strange fish in the deep, dark water that had lights on their heads, "like little flashlights to find their way in the dark." Tomás would listen as long as Uncle Díaz would talk.

Now, as he watched the brave diver leaning against the tree, Tomás recalled another one of his stories—the day Uncle Díaz had been given a diving mask. When he had put it on and gone down into the water, he had seen so clearly, he had thought he was walking in air. "I saw everything, Tomás, everything. Even the pale spots on a manta I thought was just plain."

"Uncle Díaz . . ." Tomás began; then, thinking of the great deeds the diver had accomplished, lost his nerve and could not go on.

"What can I do for you?" Uncle Díaz said, smiling and running his fingers through his hair. Tomás took courage.

"I was wondering— Once you told me about a diving mask you were given." Uncle Díaz nodded. Tomás went on. "I was wondering if I could borrow it for a few days."

Uncle Díaz leaned forward and looked more closely at Tomás.

"Are you going to dive for coral?" he asked, his eyes taking on such a luster that Tomás thought possibly he could see again.

"No, I'm going to dive for a shark—a whale shark."

"A whale shark?" Uncle Díaz repeated. "Splendid. Yes, indeed, you may borrow my mask. Wait right here, I will get it." Walking like a dancer working out some intricate choreography, he went forward, backward and then tiptoed to the next palm.

"You may borrow it," he repeated. "It's right here." He reached up as if to take the diving mask down from a hook, but before he quite found it, he slumped and sat down on the ground. Resting his head on his knees, he fell into a deep sleep.

"Oh, well," said Tomás, smiling wistfully at the sleeping hero. "I don't need a mask. I can see without one, just like you did." Miguel started the motor. Tomás splashed into the water and climbed aboard the *ponga.*

When I sell the whale shark's huge jaw, he said to himself, I will buy my very own mask.

When Miguel beached the *ponga* on Coronados Island, the pelicans were up and *kersplash*ing, and the gulls were alighting on the water beside them, trying to steal their catches from their beaks. Tomás leaped ashore and carried the food and water to the *palapa.* He went back for his spear and bag of clothes.

This is the day, he thought, looking for jobs to do to hold down his excitement. I see it in the pelican's eyes.

Tomás helped Miguel load the heavy net onto the *ponga,* glancing over his shoulder from time to time to study the submerged reef where his whale shark had been. The wind was not blowing. The water was still. The tide was in. As soon as Ramón and Miguel left and the light was bright enough, he would swim out there and observe the shark. If he could learn its habits, travel route and routine, he could lie in wait and be ready to stab it when it passed.

When the net was loaded and the water and tortillas aboard, Miguel started the Evinrude, and in minutes the *ponga* was around the south end of the island and out of sight. The sun burst over the horizon. The water turned azure blue.

Tomás picked up the palm-leaf broom and swept the sand around the *palapa* until it was smooth and clean. He would get his chores done while the sun was still too low for him to see to the bottom of the sea. Next he salted and turned the fish, gathered firewood, burned trash and filled the water bottle on the sand table. When he could find nothing more to do, he unsheathed his knife and strode over to the volcanic dyke in the next cove. There he cut a long hollow reed for a snorkel and returned to the *palapa.* He picked up his spear.

Slipping out of his clothes, Tomás walked into the sea, stuck the reed in his mouth and sat down under water. He looked around. The grebes submarined past him, chasing little fish. He saw the black legs and gold feet of a snowy egret under water. The bird was waiting patiently for a fish to come by. The reed snorkel worked; he could stay under as long as he needed to figure out the habits of the shark. Sticking the snorkel in his hair, holding his spear in his teeth, he breaststroked to the end of the reef, still several feet under water. He rested his feet upon it, adjusted his snorkel and went under.

Tomás entered the planet's fantasy world. Pink-and-lavender fan corals waved dreamily. Seaweed bucked and rippled. A bright-blue queen anglefish belted with a golden sash swam under him. The fish vanished, and a school of sunny yellow jacks wheeled into view, hung before him like a fleet of lemon spaceships and wheeled off. An oyster saw Tomás's shadow fall upon it through a rim of eye spots that reported only light and dark. The oyster closed its shell. Close by, a group of sun stars radiated silver rays in their rocky sky. The yellow jacks came back to the reef and nibbled the algae and tiny sea plants that grew there. A needlefish threaded in and out, as if it were sewing the plants together. Every creature here had a routine as well as a home. The rock reef was not only beautiful, but busy.

The daytime water creatures woke up as the sun climbed the sky. Asteroids opened their fernlike tendrils and began to eat. Dark-red sea urchins moved their stiff spines and walked—using the water for power. The seawater fell through holes in their heads and rushed down internal canals into the long, hollow spines. Valves closed behind the onrush and the spines stiffened. In stiffening, they moved. When the valves opened, the spines relaxed. Using hydraulics to stiffen and relax their spines, the sea urchins walked to find food.

Tomás could not see the whale shark, not even its tail. He decided to look in the Shallows. Still snorkeling, he kicked away from the reef, floating above stonelike limpets and dazzling mantids on the floor of the sandy sea bottom.

A puff of sand billowed up. The shark? Tomás sculled and looked down. It was not. The sand puffs outlined a huge triangular body. Giant manta, he thought as he recognized the creature, which was as big as a *palapa.* He wondered why it was on the bottom. The giant manta, the great eagle of the sea, lived at the surface, flapping its odd wings and even flying out of the water when it pleased. Was this one hiding from an enemy in the sand? Tomás took his snorkel out of his mouth and dived down toward the gentle fish. It lifted its spear-shaped tail, and from its body came a shower of little mantas that looked exactly like their mother. They had five pairs of gill slits—as do their relatives the sharks—on the lower surfaces of their bodies. Like their mother, they were shaped triangularly, with flaps around their mouths and fins that grew at the bases of their tails. Using wings, fins and tails the instant they were born, they swam off into the green gloom. They did not look back at their mother. She did not look at them. They had been born. They were.

How could Griselda say that Loreto is a pit, with all this to see? Tomás asked himself. I'll have to take her snorkeling.

Tomás turned around and kicked back to the reef. As he approached it, he saw that a huge, three-foot grouper had rendezvoused with some little damselfish. Tomás held himself still. The damselfish were eating the parasites off the back of the grouper.

Now, there you are, thought Tomás. Everybody gets something good out of that arrangement. The little fish eat, and the big fish gets cleaned.

And now I come along and wreck everything—because, big grouper, you are my mother's favorite fish.

Sticking the snorkel in his hair and holding the spear with two hands, Tomás dived and jabbed. The spear entered the grouper and came out the other side. The fish flapped and fought. Tomás held on, swimming downward. The fish was headed for the overhang. It never got that far. It turned and struggled toward the Shallows, towing Tomás. He needed air, his lungs hurt, he could not hang on much longer. He was about to let go of spear and fish when the grouper finally stopped fighting and went limp in death. Tomás lunged for the surface, a long, long way above. Gasping, he came up. He had the fish, but he had nearly drowned himself in the effort. He rolled to his back and rested, sputtering and belching air and water.

When he was breathing normally again, Tomás placed the spear and fish on his chest and kicked back to the reef. The odor of blood and the vibrations of swimming went out through the seawater and were received on sensitive living receptors under the overhang.

Just before Tomás put his feet down on the reef, he stuck the snorkel back in his mouth and looked for his shark once more. A green-gray form moved far off to his right, like a wandering planet.

"There you are," he said, his eyes smarting from the salt as he tried to see the telltale yellow spots and pointed head. He could not. He only dimly saw the caudal fin. He did not see the great hammer that separated the eyes and nostril from each other. The blur circled back, but Tomás was standing on the reef.

"I know your route," he said to the shark. "You swim under the overhang, go out toward the Shallows and come back. I am going to wait for you on the last rock when the tide is out."

He threw spear and grouper across his shoulder and, smiling happily, waded over the reef to the beach.

A Warning from a Fish and a Bird

TOMÁS put a rope through the gills of his fine grouper and swam with it out along the reef. He dived and, using a double knot, tied the fish to a rock. Even at low tide the grouper would still be underwater. He wanted to keep it fresh until he was ready to fillet it and take it home firm fleshed and sweet to his mother.

Since Ramón and Miguel would be back any time now, Tomás gave up the idea of searching for his shark and decided to catch a spiny lobster, his grandmother's favorite food, for her for Christmas.

He walked along the beach to the rocky bluff at the south end of the cove and slipped into the water. Climbing down the cliff, hand under hand, he peered into crevasses and caves where the long-tentacled delicacies lived. A chocolate-brown annelid, a tubelike sea worm with a red crown of thorns and white tentacles, pulsated below him. It was one of hundreds of species of sea worms in the Sea of Cortez that attach themselves to the rocks by using small, disc-like suckers. The mestizos did not eat them, but Tomás was sure something did. Every living thing in the sea was eaten by some other living thing, he had observed. If they were too big, like the sharks and the whales, then the tiny things got them—parasites and worms.

Tomás touched the sea worm. A fountain of water shot out of its tubelike body, and the odd-looking beast collapsed, virtually disappearing. Tomás held on to his breath and went on down the wall. The worm sucked in the sea and again stood tall. The column of water inside it acted as a very ingenious skeleton that could be ejected in a crisis.

After checking all the lobster hideouts he knew about and finding none of the occupants at home, Tomás spiraled slowly to the surface, watching the colors and the lights.

No lobsters today, he thought, and swam home across the cove, looking down on the seafloor as an eagle looks down on the land. Below him the sand rolled with the currents, and fish swam by like dream persons. Out of Tomás's line of vision the huge shark swam fitfully, thrashed and glided back to the rock reef.

Suddenly the reef-side water swirled in a vortex. Tomás lifted his head and glanced curiously in the direction of the vortex, unaware that his grouper had just been eaten. He splashed up onto the beach.

Down on the rocks of the reef where the grouper had been

tied, bits of shattered fish sank to the bottom. A red snapper fry swallowed two bites, then darted to cover in the stony cave when a grebe came after it. The frightened red snapper dropped a bite, and it sank into the seaweed. Out of the seaweed emerged a pistol shrimp that had smelled the fish. It squeezed its tail and shot upon it like a bullet, grabbing the morsel in its one huge claw.

The action was noted by a two-spotted octopus in a crevice overhead. The octopus had four eyes—two real, two false. While its true eyes focused on the shrimp, the false eyes scared off competition from above. The octopus dropped like a sock filled with stones, enveloped the shrimp and morsel in its sucker-covered arms—and ate.

Tomás walked up the beach and sat down on the warm sand. He put his chin in his hands and his elbows on his knees and pondered. The fight with the big grouper had changed his plans. He knew he would never be able to spear and land a shark.

I think I'd better snag it from the top of the reef, he thought. To do that, I'll need Ramón's big shark hook and a strong nylon line. Once I have him snagged, I'll use a reef rock as pulley and winch him up. That ought to work.

A wave rolled in carrying a dead grebe toward shore. Tomás waded out and picked it up. Its breast was riddled with a line of deep holes. He turned it over. No wounds appeared on the back.

"Shark," he said. Of all fishes, only the shark can hit with the lower jaw alone, since its jaws operate separately. A blow from one jaw, though often deadly, is relatively mild. If both jaws had come into play, there would have been no bird, just blood and scraps. Tomás studied the wound. The tooth marks were almost two inches deep.

"Big," he said, and looked out across the turquoise-blue sea. This bird had been hit by a large, toothed shark, a tiger or hammerhead. He squinted at the Shallows and wondered if it could mean that the big sharks were returning to the Tórreses' fishing grounds.

It must be so, he said to himself, a smile brightening his face. I'll tell Ramón and Miguel. This is good news. They won't have to go so far to fish.

Tomás carried the bird to the top of a sand dune and put it down. Walking back to the *palapa,* he sat down to watch the inevitable. The sky was sea blue with a scattering of powdery clouds. There were no birds flying overhead.

Hardly had he wrapped his arms around his knees than a vulture appeared high above the grebe. Tomás shook his head. He could never comprehend the magic of the vultures. Almost instantly, and from great distances, they found the dead. The scavenger was invisible one moment, then soaring over the carcass the next. How vultures knew mystified Tomás. He could understand how *águila*, the sea eagle, saw fish from great heights. They, after all, were alive and moving. But what did the vulture see—death? Stillness? Rocks were still, and they did not circle them. Did they smell the dead? Did it have an odor even a few minutes after life left it? Tomás hoped to find out someday. He regularly laid the dead on the dune, watching and trying to discover what told a vulture death had occurred. The answer was still elusive.

Yet his own senses were as keen for what he was trained to see as the vulture's. He stood up and looked out to sea. A sharp ripple had caught his eye. It was a strange boat—a chunky white inboard.

"*Oficiales,*" he said, and hoped not. People of authority frightened him. Nevertheless he rehearsed his greeting and smile.

The boat entered the cove and slowed down. Tomás could hear the men discussing something—perhaps that there were no boats on the beach, only the old rowboat that sat high and dry near the dune. Or perhaps they were saying they did not see anyone to talk to. Tomás was sitting back under the *palapa* porch in the dark shadows. He held his breath. The motor accelerated, and the boat cut a wide arc, then sped north.

As Tomás blew a sigh of relief, his attention was distracted by the reef. It was very dark, nearly purple at the end of the dyke, as if a cloud were casting a shadow. He glanced up—there was no cloud.

Tomás shook his head and rubbed his eyes. He was seeing things. The *oficiales* had made him nervous. He looked around for something to do to occupy his mind and saw that the salt bucket was almost empty. Picking up a large chunk of the salt that Miguel had purchased at the Carmen Island salt mine, he smashed it with a hammer and stuffed the pieces into the rusty salt grinder that was screwed to a heavy wooden cable spool. Energetically he turned the crank. By the time he had filled half a bucket, he had pushed the *oficiales* out of his mind and replaced them with visions of hooking his shark. He felt better.

When the bucket was full, he carried it up the dyke to the plateau where the fish were drying and resalted and turned them. The shark fins, which brought such good prices, were almost dry enough to be sold. He spread them far apart, hoping they would dry more quickly, and went on with his daydreaming.

Then, he said to himself, I will pull the shark in slowly and steadily, bracing against the rocks until I have exhausted the mammoth. I— But he did not go on. A boat came around the far end of the cove and pushed up onto the beach.

"Zoro! Jesús!" Tomás called, and ran down the beach to greet them.

"Tomás," Zoro said brusquely, "have the *oficiales* been here?" He was standing on the bow of his boat, his fur coat flapping like the wings of the manta ray.

"I saw an official-looking boat," said Tomás. "But it didn't come ashore. It went north."

Zoro's eyes bored into Tomás's, the black pupils in the yellow irises drilling like jewelers' tools.

"It went north?" Zoro's drew his lips across the tips of his sharp, uneven teeth and smiled a tricky smile.

"They are from the Fisheries Department," he said.

Tomás stepped closer.

"What are they doing?"

"They are checking nets—gill nets."

"Gill nets?" Tomás said. "Gee whiz."

All the fishermen of Loreto used gill nets, with the exception of Victorio and the sportfishermen, who used rods and reels. Some nets had finer meshes than others, and each fisherman had his own preference. A few used mesh so fine, they caught the baby tunas, marlin and yellow jacks as well as the big ones. Zoro was one of these. Ramón was not; he used a large mesh, for he knew that catching the young fish was foolish. It endangered tomorrow's catch.

"Do you think they are banning the fine gill nets?" Tomás asked. "I've heard they don't like them."

Zoro shrugged.

"Who knows? I'm not afraid of *oficiales*."

With a jerk of his head he signaled Jesús to push off, then stepped over a net with mesh so fine, a needlefish could scarcely have gotten through it.

"They are not going to stop me," he said. "I'll play fox and chicken. They go north. I go south. They go south. I go north." He laughed at the prospects of a chase. Jesús chuckled and looked up at Tomás.

"I'm glad we don't have a fish camp like you do," he said, gesturing to the *palapa*, nets, tables, anchors and cooking utensils. "We can keep moving. You're stable. You're going to get caught."

Jesús threw the motor into gear and drove off, and Zoro,

standing in the bow, pulled his ragged coat across his bare chest.

"But we don't have fine gill nets!" Tomás shouted, unheard. "So we don't have to run!"

At the end of the reef Zoro leaned over and stared into the water as intently as a great blue heron. Jesús looked back at Tomás and waved good-bye.

Jesús was a year older than Tomás and was already an experienced fisherman. He had not gone to high school. The day that school was over last June he had walked out the door into the hot sunshine and, standing legs apart, had thrown his schoolbook *Ciencias sociales tres* up in the air. He had stridden off, not looking back to see where it had fallen or even if it had struck someone as it fell. Head up, Jesús had walked toward the sea.

"Adios, José Martí," he had called out. "Adios, Fidel Castro and, also, all the presidents of Mexico. I don't have to read about any of you anymore. I am going to be a fisherman."

His exit had been grand. His shoulders had been squared and the wind had cooperated by sweeping his hair back like a genuine national hero carved out of stone. His stride had been manly. Even in Tomás's finest dreams, he was not able to carry the whale shark with the poetry of movement displayed by this young man. Nor did chickens fly up at Tomás's feet, dust rise, and dogs bark as they had when Jesús had gone to sea.

Tomás shoved his hands into his pants pockets.

I guess I should be a fisherman too, he thought.

The sanderlings ran along the water's edge, the pelicans dived for fish and three vultures were fighting over the carcass of the little grebe. Tomás did not look at any of them. For the first time, he was thinking seriously about his future. The *oficiales* had frightened him. They came from a world he did not know, and that was scary. He also did not know what high school would be like; but he did know about fishing, and he was thinking that he should begin his career right now with that shark.

He took down from the *palapa* wall an enormous hook as big as a gas can and tied a long coil of nylon line to it. Hanging them over his shoulder, he went out onto the reef.

The tide was not quite at ebb, but the reef was well above water. There were many rocks available for use as winches. Stationing himself at the end of the reef and standing as motionless as an egret, he peered into the sea.

"There you are." The dark caudal fin of the shark cast a shadow across a garden of limpets and peanut worms going about their lives on the sea bottom. The shark's head was far under the overhang, in the sweeping current that was forcing water through its gills. Tomás could see the tip of the tail, but not the head and eyes. That was good, he said to himself. I can see the shark, but the shark can't see me. He strained to catch a glimpse of the yellow spots, but the sun was in his eyes.

The angle of the sun's rays did, however, illuminate the back fin, and Tomás saw why the shark was hanging out in the swift waters along the reef. It was wounded. A great gash lay open from the base of its caudal fin to the first dorsal fin. Ramón said sharks were often cut by the propellers of boats and ships, especially the pleasant, docile sharks like the nurse and whale sharks. Some such accident had happened to Tomás's shark—and that was good. My prize is weak, he thought. He'll be easier to take.

He dropped the heavy hook and let it fall slowly until it was beside the huge tail. The whale shark was moving, but not very fast. Tomás walked along with him, jiggling the hook closer and closer to the gristly tail. When at last it was under it, Tomás yanked, felt the hook sink into the tough flesh and whipped the line around a rock. It stretched taut as the shark streaked off into the glare of the sun, roiling the water. Tomás could see nothing but spray and light. Bracing his feet against another rock, he grabbed the line and pulled. The hook sank in deeper. Tomás had his whale shark at last.

Oficiales

TOMÁS held on. If he could keep the shark from moving long enough, it would drown. The line wove back and forth as the great fish tried to swim forward. After a long while the line slackened. The shark was swimming toward the aerated water under the overhang. Tomás hauled in the slack and looped it around a rock. He took up more. Fifty feet away the water erupted as the shark took off for the deep. The line tightened. Tomás held on.

For almost an hour he managed to hold the enormous shark, knowing that eventually it must die.

Suddenly the monster stopped fighting. Tomás could almost hear the mission bells ringing for him. He pulled, gained a few inches of line and wrapped that around the rock.

The line whistled, spurted little fountains of water, stretched and broke. The shark was gone.

"Come back!" Tomás cried, and jumped into the water to swim after him. Beneath the surface he saw that rock reef was devoid of fish except for a damselfish devotedly weeding its garden. He did not have time to wonder about this as he swam down to look for the whale shark under the overhang. It was not there.

Disappointed, he surfaced and climbed up onto the reef, almost crying. Slowly he coiled the line over his shoulder. The huge hook did not come up. The line had broken; the hook was still in the gristly tail.

That'll slow him down, Tomás thought as he turned around and started home. He did not see the upthrust in the sea behind him. Widely spaced dorsal and caudal fins broke the surface—the hallmark of the dangerous hammerhead shark. It would not have mattered if he had seen it, however, for he would have seen a whale shark. Tomás believed in it.

I've got to use the spear, he said to himself on his way back to the *palapa*. I can kill the beast with it, then I can worry about landing it. He picked up his spear and returned to the reef. The tide was now at ebb, and he could see clearly to the bottom. He walked stealthily along, like the great blue heron.

"Nothing," he said when he came to the end of the reef and turned around.

A ten-foot shadow slipped in from the sea. Tomás saw it glide under the overhang out of the corner of his eye.

"There you are!" he yelled, and ran to the rocks above the spot where it had disappeared. He raised his spear. The shark was out of sight again.

"I'll swim down and spear you!" he said, but just in time he recalled his frightening battle with the grouper, a small fish by comparison with this beast, and thought better of it.

Standing alone in the afternoon light, Tomás wearily watched the reef and seafloor. A red snapper came in from the Shallows and pulled up to the reef. It offered itself to the damselfish to be groomed and cleaned of parasites. Tomás's lips curled into a big smile. Aiming a little to the side to compensate for the refraction of the water, he hurled the spear. He was his father's son. It entered the water and pierced the fish. Tomás jumped in and, with a whoop, lifted the huge skewered snapper, flapping and twisting, over his head as he swam back to the reef and climbed out.

Maybe I'll spear ten beautiful fish like this one and carry them into the plaza, he thought, pleased with himself in spite of losing the shark. He closed his eyes and conjured up the plaza and the ten flopping fish. He snorted. The vision paled beside the vision of himself with the whale shark above his head.

"But it might have to do," he said aloud, for he was now shockingly aware of the power and weight of his shark, a small one, he knew, as whale sharks go.

Returning to the beach, Tomás stopped to put the red snapper on the rope with the grouper.

"Gone," he gasped as he pulled up the empty line. Eaten. Wow, that has to be some big thing to eat a three-foot grouper. What's going on? First the grebe, then this. He frowned and looked suspiciously at the Shallows. Mysterious lights flickered off the waves. They shone purple, black and dark green. Tomás sensed the presence of evil.

"Is that you out there, Tezcatlipoca?" he asked, and shivered.

All is not well, he thought.

The motor of the *ponga* sounded in the distance, and presently Ramón and Miguel came around the tip of the island and entered the cove. When they hit the beach, Tomás was there to meet them, waving his red snapper.

"Any luck?" he asked.

"One small hammerhead and a large manta ray," Miguel answered limply. "Not so good." He brushed a lock of hair out of his face and grinned at Tomás. "But I see you did all right."

"Speared it," said Tomás proudly. "And by the way, the *oficiales* came by," he added. "But they didn't stop. Later Zoro came. He said they are checking gill nets."

"Checking gill nets?" Ramón queried. "There is no law against gill netting."

"But the *oficiales* don't like the small meshes that kill the baby fish."

"Neither do I," Ramón said with a sniff. "But that's just fine; they won't bother us," he added with relief in his voice, and leaped from the boat with agility. Tomás saw that he no longer limped. Apparently the good news about the factory boats had done wonders for Ramón, and Tomás was grateful. Ramón was the strength of the family; he must not falter or limp.

That evening Ramón rolled Tomás's red snapper in a flour batter and cooked it lightly in salt-pork fat. Tomás ate almost half of the serving, for this was his favorite meal—red snapper cooked by Ramón and eaten in the golden light before sunset.

After dinner the three Torres men gathered around a small fire just outside the sleeping-*palapa* door as they did every night before going to bed. This was the hour that Ramón and Miguel discussed politics. Tonight for the first time Tomás found himself eager to participate.

"Do the *oficiales* think the gill nets are responsible for the poor fishing?" he asked.

"Apparently so," Ramón answered. "But they ought to be out checking the shrimp boats, too. Their nets take baby fish and baby sharks and the playful little porpoises. And there are more shrimp boats than there are *pongas*."

"Why don't they?" asked Tomás, putting a twig on the fire. It flared up, illuminating their faces.

"They probably do," said Miguel. "But the shrimp industry is a wealthy one. They can pay off the *oficiales*."

"Then you should go to Mexico City and tell the Minister of Fisheries about the shrimp boats," Tomás said.

"What good would that do?" Ramón asked.

"Victorio and his wife complained to the Minister about the factory boats, and look what happened."

"We are not Victorio," said Ramón, and gently laid his hand on Tomás's knee. The gesture said, "You have a lot to learn."

Early the next morning Tomás lay wide awake, waiting in the darkness for the pelicans to *kersplash*. During the night he had figured out how to catch the shark. This was to be the great day. His success with the spear had showed him the way. He would tie a line to the spear shaft, take out the old rowboat and locate the shark. Then, like Uncle Díaz, he would jump overboard with a rock, plunge and spear him. Before the shark could do battle, he would surface, get back in the boat and tie the line to the rowboat. This time, when the whale shark tore off toward the Shallows, he would ride with it to keep the line from breaking. Eventually the shark would tire and die.

Tomás tucked his hands under his head and returned to his favorite dream. The plaza was lit with floodlights, the players in the Christmas pageant were singing and the whale shark was gleaming like a silver torpedo speckled with gold dots. At this point Tomás always conjured up the colorful details of his victory march—his clothing and the merry faces of the people.

None of them would appear for him this time, and he wondered why.

Kersplash!

Ramón and Miguel were already up. He ran to the water and dove in. The heart of Quetzalcoatl, the planet Venus, was an enormous crystal ball in the east.

The forces of good are about this day, Tomás thought as he washed. He ran to the *palapa* to dress.

"Good morning," he said to Ramón, who was pouring coffee.

"Good morning," Ramón answered, and began mixing cornmeal and lard in the palm of his hand. "The torn net is dry, Tomás. Will you help me repair it today?"

"I will," he said halfheartedly, and put off his new plan until afternoon.

"We are going to put the nets in the Shallows again," Ramón went on. "I saw several sharks there as we came through yesterday. The weather is cool. They must be seeking the warmer water."

Tomás wondered if he should tell his grandfather that the net-tearing whale shark was still about.

No, he said to himself. It's wounded. It's staying close to the reef. And with that hook in it, it will probably stay under the overhang to get oxygen.

Miguel lifted one end of the torn net and dragged it to the *palapa*. With Tomás's help he hung it from the jutting roof poles so that it was stretched out and Ramón could get to the huge tear.

Ramón brought out a box of shuttles and cords used to mend the nets and supervised Tomás while he threaded a shuttle.

"Stand beside me," he said, "and watch what I do." Ramón grasped the net with one hand and the toes of one foot, putting tension on it. With the other hand he measured off four inches of cord with the shuttle, twisted it around and made a knot. Tomás took note and, flipping his shuttle, knotted his cord too. He worked more slowly than his grandfather, but his knots were almost as tight and even. He was very pleased with himself and bent into his work with concentration, not even thinking of his shark. Being fourteen was doing more for him than filling out the muscles of his body and growing fuzz on his lip. It was also turning him into a worker.

Late in the morning the mended net was loaded onto the *ponga,* and Tomás climbed aboard to help Miguel set it in the Shallows. Ramón took the helm.

As the boat glided past the end of the reef, Tomás stood on the bow and looked for his whale shark. Brightly colored fish were swarming over the reef again, but the shark was not to be seen.

"Drop the net anchor, Tomás," Ramón called when they were over the deepest water. Tomás tossed over the rusty thing and listened to its rope mumble as it unwound.

"Now the net," said Ramón. Tomás dumped the net overboard. Weights on the bottom carried it to the seafloor. Styrofoam floats pulled up the top until it was stretched fully open.

"The buoy, Miguel," called Ramón. While Tomás kept feeding out the net, Miguel tossed an empty five-gallon plastic water barrel overboard—and one end of the net was set and marked. Ramón eased the *ponga* slowly along while Tomás and Miguel strained and heaved as they let out the remainder of the heavy mesh. Three hundred feet from the first marker, Ramón pulled the net taut with the boat and Tomás dropped the other anchor and buoy. The Tórreses' net was ready for sharks.

"Miguel," Ramón said, pulling on the rudder and sending the boat into a turn, "we are going to Carmen Island to bring in the other net. Tomorrow we go home for Christmas."

The *ponga* rode smoothly over the blue-green water. Tomás sat on the deck of the bow, legs crossed, head back, letting the sweet air blow over his ruddy cheeks and bronze skin. His lips curled into a peaceful smile. There was nothing before him but the endless sea and sky. He closed his eyes. The life of a fisherman had a spiritual dimension.

I like it, he said to himself, and forgot everything but the wind and spray on his body and the wide spaces before him.

I like it, he said again when they were pulling in the net.

The net secured in the *ponga,* Miguel took the helm and Tomás stretched out on the big, bulky net beside Ramón. Their faces were expressionless and listless. The take was only one large manta.

As they entered the cove, a boat came around the north end of the island, headed their way. Presently they could see Jesús at the helm and Zoro standing in the bow, his fur coat rippling like that of a fox on the run.

Miguel waved and pulled alongside them.

"The *oficiales* are going south," Zoro called, his white face scored by the dark lines around his grin. "I'm going north." Jesús laughed, swung the boat outward and gave it gas.

Ramón shook his head and smiled.

"He's in a hurry, all right."

"They'll never catch Zoro," Tomás commented. "Jesús said his grandfather was a pirate. He taught him all the secret coves and bays around Loreto."

Laughing good-humoredly as they watched Zoro disappear into the rising wind and waves, the Torres fishermen headed on home with the birds. The vultures were gliding toward Loreto, the gulls and plovers flying seaward to their rendezvous at sea. The dainty Forster's terns sped northward toward a deserted rock island, and the frigate birds, now a large gathering of black crosses high in the sky, were sailing to their mangrove islets along the mainland shore.

As Miguel beached the *ponga,* Tomás glanced back to look for his shark. A boat was racing along the horizon, and it was not Zoro going north. It was the government boat.

"Here comes the *oficiales,*" he said, and jumped to the sand.

Ramón, Miguel and Tomás stood perfectly still as the large boat puttered into the cove and pulled up in deep water by the reef.

Two men in uniform got out. The Tórreses walked across the sand to meet them, smiling cordially.

"Welcome," Ramón said with dignity.

"Good evening," said the taller of the two men. "My name is Ignacio, this is Luís." The voice was severe. Tomás felt his heart race. But everything would be all right. Ramón was a shark fisherman. His nets did not catch baby fish.

"You own this *palapa*?" Ignacio asked.

"Yes, sir," Ramón answered, his voice betraying his pride in his fishing camp.

"We are here for the government's tourism bureau—FONATUR." Ramón's smile slipped away. This was not what he had expected to hear. What did tourism have to do with the size of nets? Tomás stepped closer to Ramón.

"As you know, the government is developing Loreto as a big tourist center"—Ignacio went on—"the hotel, the airport. Loreto has many attractions—Our Lady of Loreto Mission, the museum, the prehistoric cave paintings on the road to the ancient San Javier Mission in the mountains, not to mention Puerto Escondido."

Tomás had never been to Puerto Escondido, which was only twenty miles away, but he knew it was important. A beautiful, nearly landlocked bay, its crystalline waters were world famous for their good fishing and spectacular scuba diving.

"And," proceeded Ignacio, "there is Coronados Island." He gestured to the pure white beach, the blue waters and graceful volcano. "Beautiful."

Ramón stood as straight as a spear. He scarcely blinked.

The *oficial* seemed to be waiting for him to comment. When he did not, he went on.

"We don't want to move you off the island," he said, "because you're an old man and have been coming here for many years. But this is government property. The island belongs to the Mexican people.

"We have decided you can stay if you pay rent." Ramón did not say a word. He remained standing regally, his head lifted, listening and looking into the man's eyes.

"If you would like to come with me," Ignacio went on, "we'll go to the tourism office in Loreto. You can sign the papers and pay there."

"How much?" asked Miguel with iron tones.

"We don't know. The Minister has to decide," said Luís, who had been making a tour of the camp and had now returned. He rocked back on his heels. "I see," he said, "that you fillet your fish and throw the carcasses in the next cove for the gulls and vultures. This will have to stop. The odor offends the tourists. They come here to picnic. They don't like the smell."

Miguel stepped forward, folding his arms on his chest. Ignacio changed the subject. "What kind of nets do you use?" he asked pleasantly.

"Shark nets," Miguel answered coldly. "They do not kill the small fish."

"Victorio and the other sportfishermen want the Fisheries Department to stop all commercial fishing around Loreto," Luís said. "The fish are disappearing."

"They take a lot themselves," Ramón said. "Hundreds of big-game fish a day."

Ignacio did not reply.

"As we all know," went on Luís, "the Japanese factory boats are the main reason why there are not many fish anymore. But they are gone. Now we must try to rebuild the fish populations. Tourists will be coming to Loreto primarily to fish. We want their dollars."

"But we are shark fishermen," said Miguel. "We do not take the game fish."

"Shark fishing with rod and reel," said Ignacio knowingly, "is becoming a very popular sport with the wealthy Americans. And the Baja shark population is very low. Too many of you commercial fishermen.

"But don't worry about that. There are no laws about who fishes where and for what." He smiled and slapped Ramón across the shoulder. Ramón's face was iron.

"You know what I'm going to do?" Ignacio said with a condescending edge to his voice. "I'm not going to take you into the office today. It is almost Christmas. Why don't you come in next week at your convenience?"

Ramón did not thank his visitors, nor did he help push them off into the sea, as was his custom. They were grounded on the reef, but he simply stood, head up, shoulders back, as the *oficiales* took off their shoes and socks, rolled up their pressed pant legs and waded into the water. Grunting and yelling instructions to each other, they finally got the boat off the reef by themselves, crawled aboard and sped away.

Tomás could feel terror in the air. He could not take in all the implications of the *oficiales'* visit, but he knew one thing—Ramón could not pay rent.

"This beach is ours," Tomás said. "The land distribution act said that a man owns the land he lives and works on."

"Not beaches, Tomás," Ramón said softly. "They belong to us all, and they are free."

"What can we do?" Tomás asked. "Will the governor of Baja help us? You voted for him."

Ramón slipped his arm around Tomás's shoulders and drew him to him.

"Go to high school, Tomás," he said. "This way of life is over. I do not know what comes next, but you must find out for us."

The Return of Quetzalcoatl and Tezcatlipoca

UNCLE DÍAZ was sitting under the date palm when the Tórreses came home Christmas Eve. Their luck had been better that morning. The net in the Shallows brought in three hammerheads, a large baracuda and a nice red snapper. Ramón had filleted the snapper for a holiday treat and wrapped it in salt grass. Tomás lifted it carefully out of the *ponga.*

"Tomás, here," called Uncle Díaz, getting steadily to his feet. "I found it. I found my diving mask." His face was freshly shaven, and his eyes seemed to glitter with sight. He held up the black mask with its wide window, and Tomás stuffed the snapper into his clothing bag and ran to meet him.

"That's a very good mask," Tomás said. "I saw one like it in the dive shop. It cost many hundred thousand pesos."

"Are you really going to hunt for a whale shark?" Uncle Díaz asked, smiling broadly, his teeth shining white under his neatly trimmed mustache. He leaned close to hear Tomás's answer.

"I've changed my mind," he shouted. "He's awful big. I think I will spear him from a boat. But thank you very much."

"A whale shark," Uncle Díaz went on as if he had not heard Tomás. "Now, that would be fun to dive for." He blinked and rubbed his eyes. "Where is it?"

"Off Coronados Island, under the overhang of the rock reef. It's injured. A boat propeller, I think. It has been there for several days—healing itself."

"It would be better to spear it from under the water. We could swim up beside it and hit the heart," suggested Uncle Díaz. "No struggle or fight if we hit the heart. Together we could manage."

"We?" Tomás's face brightened, and then he dreamed. He was underwater with Uncle Díaz, the legendary coral diver. They were spinning through the green-blue water, their spears at their sides, schools of glittering fish escorting them to the shark. The mission bells were ringing for them.

"I'll go get another mask," Uncle Díaz said. "We'll locate him and leap from the boat. You come from this direction, I come from that direction, and we drive it under the overhang. I can see us now. A million pretty fish shining like jewels around us. We see the shark, moving, moving; its round eyes find us, but we are faster, we aim for it like bullets." Uncle Díaz smiled as he, too, dreamed of better worlds and circumstances.

"Let's go tomorrow afternoon when the tide is ebbing," he

went on. "There won't be many fishermen out on Christmas Day. We can work undisturbed."

"We'll have to use Grandpapa's little *ponga*," Tomás said, gesturing toward the family's old boat anchored out in the water. "The big *ponga* will be high and dry in the afternoon."

"The little *ponga* is too small for a whale shark. We'll use my brother's," Uncle Díaz said. "It's always anchored out. He lets me borrow it when I'm sober." Tomás glanced at him. That's what it was that made him different today. Uncle Díaz had not been drinking. Not only had his appearance changed, but it was true that his vision was better. He had seen the little *ponga*, which was quite far away.

"Here is your mask," Uncle Díaz said. Tomás hugged it to his chest, picked up his clothing bag and, seeing Ramón and Miguel far up the dusty street, took Uncle Díaz's hand and guided him toward the Morélloses' casa.

José, who had been waiting for Tomás to come home, saw him approaching with Uncle Díaz and ran to meet them, grinning triumphantly.

"Tomás," he called, "I did it. I made the Roman candle."

"Did you really, José?" Tomás was impressed. José's dream was about to come true.

"Of course I did. I followed Uncle López's instructions right down to the final period."

"I hope so," said Uncle Díaz. "Fireworks are very dangerous." Tomás nodded.

"We'll set it off right after the Christmas pageant in the plaza," José said.

"The pageant starts at ten o'clock," Tomás informed him. "What time do you want to go?"

"Meet me at the crossroads at nine thirty." Tomás agreed. José opened the gate to his casa, then turned to his uncle.

"Uncle Díaz," he said, "Dad is ready to kill the fiesta pig. He's been trying to find you. He needs your help."

"Tell him I'm coming," said Uncle Díaz, lingering to speak to Tomás.

José, still grinning, ran down the path to the brick cave.

"Tomás," Uncle Díaz said, "it will be a beautiful thing to bring up a whale shark. Everyone will cheer and clap. One has not been taken for many years."

"Yes," said Tomás. "But mostly I want it for my grandfather." Tomás paused. What had he said? Where was the scene at the plaza? He could not conjure it up. Instead of banners and dancing people, he saw the *oficiales*, their grim faces threatening the Tórreses' way of life.

"We may lose our camp. Have you heard?"

"Yes." Uncle Díaz nodded. "I did hear. The *oficiales* were here this morning. No more fish camps on the islands without paying rent."

"A whale shark would bring a lot of pesos, would it not?" Tomás asked him hopefully.

"Yes, yes. How big did you say it was?"

"Maybe ten feet—not big for a whale shark. But I've not really gotten a good look at it."

"A ten-footer would pay the rent for many months," Uncle Díaz said.

"Will you really help me?" Tomás asked, his voice low and urgent.

"I will help you." He smiled and fumbled for Tomás's hand. "I love Ramón very much. He is a fine man."

"Where and when shall we meet?"

"On the fishermen's beach," he said. "At two o'clock on Christmas Day."

"I'll be there," Tomás promised. He watched the famous diver walk steadily down the path to the palm where the pig was tied.

Tomás's heart was racing with excitement when he caught up with Ramón and Miguel. As he fell in stride beside them, he made an effort to see himself holding the shark over his head. He could not.

The Tórreses' noisy, happy homecoming turned instantly silent when Ramón told his family the news.

"A rental fee for the island?" Dolores sat down on a chair. "But it is ours. We have been there fifty years." She pressed her hands together. "It is hard enough to make the pesos stretch now, with inflation going up and up," she said. "How can we pay rent?" Ramón sat down beside her and put his arm around her shoulder.

"It is Christmas Eve," he said. "Let us be happy. We will worry about the *oficiales* another day, and then another and yet another." He laughed with genuine joy and lifted his arms above his head. Dolores smiled bravely.

Miguel and Digna were standing under the *palapa* porch, holding hands.

"I'm frightened," Digna whispered, tightening her grip. Miguel pushed a few loose hairs from her face and kissed her round, plump cheek.

"Things will work out," he said. "The Lady of Guadalupe is taking care of us." Digna glanced at the altar that Francisca and María had made and fervently hoped she was. Miguel kissed her again and, hurrying to his box of personal belongings in the sleeping *palapa*, opened it and took out a bottle of wine. Placing two empty mustard glasses on the blue table, he filled them, one for Ramón and one for himself.

"It's Christmastime," he said. "Let us be happy. To the Lady of Guadalupe." He lifted his wine glass high.

"To the birth of the Christ child," said Ramón, touching his glass to Miguel's. Each took a small sip and sat down at the table. The women joined them, drinking coffee. Good mestizo women did not drink alcohol; nor did good mestizo children.

María, who had been visiting friends, ran down the path to the patio, her curly hair bouncing, her cheeks red with excitement. She plopped herself down beside Tomás.

"The Christ child has come to us," she said, pointing to three prettily wrapped presents under the portrait of the Lady of Guadalupe. "Come see." She pulled him from the table to the presents.

"Read me the names, Tomás, please," she said.

"This big one is for you, María." He pointed to her name, which his mother, the only woman in the house who could read and write, had carefully printed on the box.

"And I get this one. Olé!" Tomás leaned over a large rectangular present and sucked in his breath. Then he looked at the third gift.

"'For Tomás,'" he read. "Hey, I get this one too." He was both surprised and pleased. This was the first year his family had adopted the U.S. custom of giving gifts at Christmas, a custom that was just beginning to become popular in Loreto.

Seeing his name on the presents made Tomás feel very special. As this pleasure trickled through him, he felt a larger pleasure, one so satisfying that he could not believe its power. He was going to give a gift for the first time in his life. He felt as if he were breathing beneath the sea.

"When do we open them, Tomás?" María asked.

Francisca got up from the table and slipped her arms over María's shoulder.

"Not until tomorrow," she said. "That's when the three kings gave their gifts to the baby."

It wasn't, Tomás recalled, but he didn't care. He felt wonderful—Uncle Díaz was going to dive with him, and they would kill the whale shark, carry it to the plaza—and pay the rent.

After a late dinner Tomás dressed in his best red pants and a red-and-orange striped shirt. He combed his hair neatly and brushed his teeth thoroughly under the hose.

"I'm going to the pageant," he called to his mother, and hurried down the path. As he swung out the gate, he set himself to dreaming, as he always did, but could not bring a vision to mind. The trees and dusty road were all he saw.

Something strange is happening to me, he thought. First I can't see the plaza, then I can't see the people, and now I can't see my gold clothes anymore. He tried again. His red pants remained red, his shirt orange and red.

He gave up.

José was waiting for him under the streetlight at the intersection. A long cylinder with a pointed top and a stick at the other end was tucked under his arm. José's dream was about to come true. Tomás thought about Uncle Díaz's warning and hoped nothing would go wrong. As they came to the arroyo, Bruja trotted from under a bougainvillea vine and took his position at Tomás's heels.

"Bruja," Tomás said, "stay home. José is going to blow off his rocket. You'll jump out of your skin." José laughed joyously, and Bruja came along.

Outside the open-air Café Olé, a small restaurant where gringos and Mexicans met, Tomás and José stopped. Salsa music, a jazzy mix of electric guitars and drums, was coming from a radio on the kitchen counter. Tomás bumped his hips and snapped his fingers in time to the music. José gave him a shove. Bruja stopped and sat down beside a man eating tostados.

The boys passed streetlight posts coiled with crepe paper and stores filled with tinsel and lights. Plastic flowers brightened windows. The street was already crowded with men, women and children dressed in the latest American fashions via Hong Kong. Boys bounced balls on the ends of long rubber bands, and a group of girls and their mothers carried a large, parrot-shaped piñata. They were on their way to a party and talked excitedly about the gifts that would fall out of the papier-mâché bird when it was finally broken by the blindfolded children, swinging sticks.

Loreto is certainly not a pit tonight, Tomás said to himself. Even the Morellos home, with its piles of rubbish and dismantled cars, looked pretty. Over and around the cars hung brightly colored dresses and pants on the laundry lines. They flapped like medieval banners.

Tomás thought of the rental fee, but even that could not make him sad. It was Christmas Eve in Loreto.

At the plaza they sat down on the low wall that encircled it and watched the singers and actors who would soon be putting on the pageant. All were dressed in seventeenth-century religious costumes that were more Aztec than Christian. They were chatting and laughing beside a low stage that had been erected for the performance. Tomás wandered over to them, then stood still and stared. Until this night he had not realized that the actors and singers were ordinary people. Two of the soldiers were Tomás's neighbors. The hermit was Juan Fuertes, his science teacher, and the boy angel was the knobby-kneed son of the chief of the police. The devils, with their black hoods, horns and long red tongues, who had scared him to death last year, were, he saw, the baker and the owner of the ice house.

"Feliz Navidad," someone said, tugging at his sleeve, and Tomás turned around to see Griselda and her aunt, Victorio's wife.

"Aunt Bárbara," Griselda said, "this is my schoolmate Tomás Torres. Tomás, this is my aunt."

"How do you do?" Tomás said respectfully.

"Are you Ramón Torres's grandson?" the well-dressed woman asked.

"Yes, I am."

"He's a very fine fisherman," she said, then knitted her brow. "But I am sorry to hear about the *oficiales*. Tell him he can work for us."

"Victorio will be here soon," said Griselda. "He wants to make Ramón an offer."

No way, thought Tomás. Ramón would never be a sportfishing guide. He was a commercial fisherman who netted food for the people, like the fishermen in the days of Jesus and Quetzalcoatl.

"Thank you," he said. "But everything is going to turn out all right."

Tomorrow he and Uncle Díaz would be under the sea, spears in hand, swimming toward the whale shark.

"The offer is good anytime," Aunt Bárbara said. "Tell him to think it over. The tips are very good."

Griselda and her aunt stopped talking. The actors and singers had taken their places on the stage, under an elaborate canopy decorated with bright bells, ribbons, tinsel and flowers.

"Let's get closer, Aunt Bárbara," Griselda said, and she led the way through the jostling crowd to the front row.

They are very different women, Tomás mused. I wonder if all the women in Mexico City are like them. Why, they even came here alone, without Victorio escorting them.

José grabbed him by the shoulder.

"I've found just the spot for the Roman candle," he said. "The unfinished fountain bowl in the lower plaza has sand in it. We can stand the rocket—" But he did not finish. The violinist struck a chord, albeit off-key. The pageant had begun.

"A child has been born," said the angel, who was the policeman's son, dressed like Quetzalcoatl, in a white pleated skirt with a cascade of gold feathers shooting out of a silver crown.

"Follow the star," sang the performers as they took three steps forward, pivoted and took three steps back. This went on for a long, long time.

Tomás worked his way to the front of the crowd. He wanted to see the two devils tempt the hermit, Juan Fuertes. First they offered him gold, then a talking bird and a fine house. The hermit was sorely tempted and even turned to follow the devils. Tomás held his breath. Fortunately, the Quetzalcoatl figure stood up, and just in time. The hermit saw him, recognized his goodness and walked away from the devils. Holding up his arms in supplication, he marched toward the star. The audience cheered. Next the devils tempted the soldiers, and they too almost succumbed. But the angel prevailed, and they turned away from temptation.

The battles between evil and good grew more and more intense; swords clashed, the music mounted and finally two of Tomás's classmates, who were dressed like nuns, pleaded and called the travelers on to righteousness. And then came the climax: Quetzalcoatl, the angel, arose and pointed to the child in the crib behind him. Upon seeing the child, the devils ran off and all the performers fell to their knees. Good had won.

"Good," said Tomás aloud and with deep satisfaction.

"What?" said José, who had slipped up beside him. "You don't take this dumb thing seriously, do you? It's just an old, old play. The Jesuit monks thought it up to entertain the people on Christmas Eve so they would give more money to the padres." He laughed. "Let's go. We've got to get down to the fountain."

Tomás ducked around a family of gringos and followed José. The pageant was, indeed, over. Radios and cassette players were blaring, and carts laden with burritos, tamales and soda pop appeared at the edges of the crowd.

"This way," said José, carefully protecting his Roman candle from the elbows of passersby. Tomás grabbed José's shirttail so he would not lose him.

"Tomás!" a man called. He let go of José and turned around. Juan Fuertes, the hermit and his science teacher, was coming his way, still in his long white costume, with clay skulls dangling from his belt.

"Tomás," Juan said as they met. "We have not heard your decision about going on to high school. The papers must be filed soon. I hope you are going."

"I am still thinking about it," Tomás answered. "My grandfather wants me to, but things have taken a bad turn. I must earn money for the family—and besides, I'm getting to be a good fisherman."

"Tomás," Juan Fuertes said forcefully, "you are a gifted student. You must not waste your mind. You could be a first-rate biologist and help Mexico solve some of these fishing problems."

Tomás stood still. Yesterday, after the *oficiales* had departed, Ramón had convinced him to go to school. Now he wanted to fish. Uncle Díaz was going to teach him how to hold his breath and dive deep. Uncle Díaz would teach him how to spear whale sharks, and Tomás would bring lots of pesos home to Ramón and his mother.

Apparently Juan Fuertes was reading his mind.

"Tomás," he said, "do you remember how excited you were when you read about the work of Charles Darwin and Louis Pasteur in our textbook? Remember the long talks we had about Madame Curie?"

"Yes, I do," he answered. "Would high school teach me to be a scientist?"

"You would be on your way," Juan replied. "There is a great need for biologists in Mexico. We need to study our land and waters so we can preserve them. We need to study the fish and keep them producing food for our tables."

"Could I do that?"

"You could," Juan answered.

"Tomás!" José called. "Tomás! Hurry!"

Tomás ran toward José, hesitated and turned back to his teacher. He was seeing a magical new dream. It was one of books and papers like the priest's quarters. A laboratory like Madame Curie's floated down onto the deck of Charles Darwin's *Beagle.* Fish poured from the sea, sharks multiplied a thousandfold and grew enormous. He shook his head as a new world flowered before him. Then he thought about the rent.

"I just don't know," he said to his teacher. "I am very confused and mixed up."

"Come talk to me before the holidays are over," Juan Fuertes said. "Or I'll come to your casa. You must not waste your mind. Anyone can fish."

Tomás took a few steps toward José and stopped. "You must not waste your mind," he said to himself.

Suddenly an explosion rent the air. Tomás looked up. A streak of fire was burning upward through the night. Sparklets of light fell from it like shooting stars. High above the mission tower the streak turned into a glowing ball of blue fire. *Boom!* Red-and-yellow sprays shot out and burned up against the black velvet of the night.

"José," whispered Tomás. "Oh, José, you did it. It's beautiful."

"Who set that off?" asked Juan Fuertes, who was standing nearby.

"José. José Morellos. Isn't it super? He made it."

"Well, he has a calling," said the teacher with a grin. "The government fireworks industry will certainly want him to come work for them."

"That's what he wants to be," said Tomás. "A firecracker artist, a pyrotechnician."

After a brief hush, the stunned but delighted rocket watchers found their voices and cheered. Tomás looked around for José; and suddenly there he was coming toward him, high above everyone's head, held aloft by members of the high-school soccer team. He was an airplane, an *águila,* everything that soared and was looked up to. He was carried to the middle of the plaza, where a yellow spotlight played over him. High above the crowd, laughing with happiness, wobbled José, looking as golden as Quetzalcoatl.

"The play is right," Tomás said to Juan Fuertes. "Good does win over evil." He thanked his teacher for his advice and ran off to join José.

"Tomás," Juan Fuertes called after him, "will you come and talk to me?"

"Yes, Señor," he called. "As soon as I get Grandpapa his Christmas present."

Three Gifts

THE bells *dingdong*ed, calling the people of Loreto to midnight Mass. Firecrackers snapped, and the spicy odor of chili mixed with the sweet scents of cornmeal and hot peppers. Mariachi music throbbed across the plaza, and the three-hundred-year-old church slowly filled. Candlelight illumined the brilliant red-, blue- and gold-painted carvings of the altar at the end of the long, narrow nave. The surface of the massive plastered walls was irregular, the ceiling very high. Tomás and José were not going to attend Mass. The Tórreses and Morélloses were religious but casual about attendance, particularly the boys.

Tomás made his way to the platform where the soccer team had carried José, but could not find him. Wandering in and out among jubilant friends and strangers, he arrived at the stone wall and sat down. The words of Señor Fuertes kept haunting him and forcing him to think about his problem. Should I be a fisherman or a student? he asked himself.

He had to decide soon, but it was becoming harder and harder to do so. Tomás cast his eyes to the ground and dreamed his own version of the Christmas pageant. The *ponga* and the shark nets were battling Charles Darwin's sailing ship, the *Beagle*. The bumphead parrotfish and the damselfish fought shelves of books.

Good will prevail, he thought. I'll just have to wait and see. He sat up straight and scratched his head. But which one is the good? The fisherman or the student?

He glanced back over the stage. Good and evil had been so simple and obvious in the church pageant. It did not take much thought to see the difference between the devils and the saints; but what about the difference between school and fishing? It was not so clear which one was good and should win. Time was running out, Señor Fuertes had said. He had to make a choice. Tomás rubbed his head, got to his feet and ran in and out of the crowd to both find and lose himself.

He came to a stop at the steps leading down to the lower plaza. José had returned to the fountain and was studying the charred remains of his rocket. Two little boys were watching him in wide-eyed admiration.

"José!" Tomás called, and ran down the steps, threw his leg over the unfinished fountain bowl and slid on his pants to the bottom.

"Good! Good! José," he said, "you are a real pyrotechnician. The best."

"Did you see it?" José asked. "You didn't come with me."

"I saw it. Everyone saw it."

José's face was black with soot from the gunpowder that had launched the rocket, but he was grinning.

"It would have been much prettier," he said, "if I had made the streamers explode streamers. Two waterfalls of light would have been sensational."

"It was perfect, José," Tomás said. "As if heaven had opened and celebrated the stars."

"I can make double streamers, Tomás," José went on. "I know how. Come help me. You can read the directions while I pack the chemicals." He dropped the ashes of his rocket and brushed his dirty hands on his pants. "Did you convince Ramón to give you a shark's jaw? I need more black powder."

Tomás nodded and smiled. "A nice one, with lots of teeth."

"Good. I have a man to buy it. Do I still get a seller's fee?"

"Yes, but not so much this time." He leaned toward him. "I'm saving for a diver's mask." José rocked back on his heels and smiled at him.

"So you are going to be a fisherman. That's great."

"José!" Victorio was standing on the plaza wall above them, his feet spread wide. "I've been looking for you. Don't go. Wait." He ran down the steps and crossed to the fountain, his pink trousers glowing red in the floodlights.

"José," he said, pushing back his broad-rimmed Stetson hat, "you have a future. Pyrotechnics is a good business. Come to my casa after Christmas. Let's talk about starting a little fireworks business here in Loreto. I'll finance it. You make the fireworks. I sell them, and I give you part of the profits."

José climbed up out of the fountain bowl and stood before Victorio, his thumbs stuck in his pockets like a business dealer.

"Thank you, sir," he said. "But I am going to the mainland to work with my uncle. I need to learn a lot more."

"Perhaps," Victorio said. "But it seems to me you know enough already for a nice little business. We could do well here. People have to go all the way to La Paz for fireworks now. Think of all the church fiestas that require fireworks—six, or is it seven?—and there are all the political fiestas too."

"I do like to make rockets," José said, wiping his sooty forehead. "I really do, but I—" Victorio interrupted before José could say no.

"Think my offer over and come see me. The mainland is very far from your family."

"Yes, it is," José replied thoughtfully.

"You can have all the combustibles you need." He slapped José on the back.

"Tomás," José turned to his friend, "what do you think?"

"It's kind of dangerous if you don't know what you're doing. I—"

"Come see me," said Victorio in a booming voice that drowned out Tomás. Hastily he turned and walked off.

"Tomás," José said excitedly, "I could buy chemicals right away. I won't have to wait until the shark's jaw dries."

"That's true," Tomás said thoughtfully. "But maybe you will never learn how to make that star that will burst into quetzal birds if you don't go study with your uncle."

"Maybe I wouldn't," said José. "And I do want to make quetzal birds. Let me think. But, wow, free pesos to buy chemicals with."

"It sure is tempting," Tomás agreed as together they mounted the steps to the upper plaza to mingle with the other people who were not at Mass. A mariachi singer with a fine bushy mustache was crooning a love song to an American family, and one of the pageant devils was eating tostados and drinking Coca-Cola by his family's cook cart. His mother was pointing him out to passersby and proudly mouthing the words "My son, my son."

As Tomás and José neared the cart, the devil, who had taken off his black robe and horned cap, recognized José.

"Firecracker man," he said, grabbing José's hand and shaking it. "You did a good job. Next year make it even bigger."

One of the pretty pageant nuns joined the devil, smiling at José.

"You are really clever," she said, pushing back her curled locks and tucking her chin shyly. "I don't know how you do it." José beamed immodestly.

"I can make an even more beautiful rocket," he said, and threw out his chest. Tomás knew his friend well. This conversation was going to go on and on. He ambled over to the plaza wall and sat down.

Through the church door he could see the Lady of Guadalupe in her gold frame high above the altar. Below her the padre, dressed in robes of white silk, stood like a saint himself, bowing behind a gold-painted trestle that read YO SOY EL PAN DE VIDA—"I am the bread of life." The choir chanted, the altar bells tinkled. Tomás gazed at the Lady of Guadalupe, hoping she might help him in his confusion, but no word came from on high.

"I'll know tomorrow," he said, glancing at José, who was still talking to the pretty girl in the white robe. Tomás scrunched up his face and headed home. Tomorrow, he thought, should decide something. Uncle Díaz and I will be soaring with the giant mantas. We'll float above the sea hares and sand dollars on the seafloor. I should know after that. He darted past the Café Olé, and Bruja joined him again.

A mind should not be wasted, he heard again, and broke into a run to get away from the voice.

Christmas morning dawned cool. A few clouds covered the eastern sky, speaking of a conflict between warm and cold air. Tomás got up moments before Gallo crowed, only to find Dolores and his mother already in the kitchen, preparing the Christmas feast.

María climbed out of the bed and stood restlessly while Digna slipped a white dress over her head and zipped it up the back. It was trimmed with lace ruffles. Although it was made of cheap nylon and many of the seams were fraying, to Tomás it looked like an angel's robe, and María a red-cheeked angel. No sooner was she dressed than she sat down beside her present and watched to make sure it did not go away. Tomás fixed her a bowl of cornflakes, but she would not eat.

María's excitement tingled through everyone, but especially Digna, so when Ramón got up, she begged her mother-in-law to awaken the rest of the family. Dolores glanced at the impatient María and smiled. She picked up and rang a small clay bell, a present from her long-ago wedding, when she had been fourteen.

In a very few minutes everyone was standing under the palm porch roof before the Lady of Guadalupe. Ramón took his seat, then Miguel and Dolores. The daughters-in-law sat on the earthen floor behind Tomás and María. Francisca lit the candles below the Christmas altar.

Tomás wished he had the shark to give to his grandfather right now. But it would be all right. This afternoon would still be Christmas. He measured the distance between the date palm and the lemon trees. The shark would fit there nicely.

With a grandfatherly smile Ramón got to his feet and presented María her gift. She tore it open without breathing.

"A doll!" she blurted joyfully. Hugging the pink-and-white doll with gold hair, she lunged for Digna's lap and buried her head in the folds of her skirt.

"Do you like it?" Digna asked, her plump hands caressing the curly head.

"Yes, yes." María sat up and gazed at her beautiful doll, whose arms and legs moved up and down. The doll was dressed in white, like herself.

"Help me, Mommy Digna," María said. "Dolly is hungry. She wants a burrito." María rolled her *r*'s so long that Ramón and Tomás burst out laughing and Francisca covered her mouth in glee.

Now it was Tomás's turn. He tore the paper from the larger present and let it fall to the ground.

"A fishing tackle box!" he gasped, then looked from face to face in astonishment. "My own tackle box."

"Mother," he said, turning to her. "Did you give me this?" She did not answer. "It is wonderful. Now I have a tackle box like Grandpapa and Miguel." Francisca nodded, and Tomás opened the box. Lying on the top layer was a colorful assortment of hooks, lures and spinners. On the bottom layer were various fishing lines and tools. Tomás looked from face to face to discover who had given it.

"It was your father's," Francisca finally said, pressing her hands to her cheeks and squeezing back tears. "It is time for you to use it. I give it to you with love."

Tomás was deeply moved as he looked upon the things that had been touched and used by the father he did not remember. Thoughtfully he picked up each hook and spinner and turned it over in his hand. As he studied each fishing line, he suddenly realized the tackle box was a message from his mother. She wanted him to become a fisherman.

His grandfather was looking at him. I do not give you this gift, his eyes said.

Ramón did, however, have a present for him. He passed Tomás the other box. In it was a pair of new pants. "School pants?" Tomás asked, and looked at his grandfather. He nodded.

The giving was over. Dolores lit the fire, and presently the pungent odors of spices and frying fish filled the air.

The Christmas feast was paraded to the table. Digna carried in salsa, spiced vegetables, sugar rolls, tortillas and a bowl of refried beans. Dolores brought out a red ceramic bowl of rice, and Francisca took a chicken out of an oven of clay and placed it ceremoniously at Miguel's place.

"I hope that is not Gallo," said Tomás, "or I will never get up in the morning." María and Ramón laughed, and Digna smiled as she arranged fresh tomatoes, bright yellow-green lemons, oranges and pomegranates in the center of the feast.

By the time Dolores had placed the herb-drenched snapper on the table, she did not have to call anyone to dinner. They were all seated.

"Ramón," she said, "it's time to pray."

"Lady of Guadalupe," he said, crossing himself, "we thank you."

"And take care of us," Dolores added. "We need your help. Amen."

For two hours the Torres family feasted, laughed and forgot their problems. Miguel poured himself and Ramón the last of his bottle of wine and, between sips, teased Tomás about Griselda. He had seen them walking to school together. Tomás blushed and said Miguel's mustache needed trimming, then jumped from the table. Miguel chased him around the bean tree and back. Tomás laughed, his infectious haw-haws ringing through the casa grounds and tickling even serious Digna to laughter.

When Tomás sat down, María crawled into his lap, and she fed her doll a bit of everything while the family told stories. Francisca told about finding the cactus fruit, and Ramón recalled how he had once started the *ponga* too fast and sent Miguel flying head over heels into the water—and no one mentioned the *oficiales.*

When the sun had passed the meridian and was descending toward afternoon, Tomás grew restless. He did not know how to leave the table and meet Uncle Díaz. Then María again ran up with her doll.

"You be the daddy, Tomás," she said. "And I'll be the mommy. This is the baby."

"Okay," he said, getting to his feet. "Mommy, you take care of the baby. I must go fishing." He picked up the cardboard box his new pants had come in.

"This is the baby's bed," he said. "Put her to sleep while I am gone."

María put the doll in the box and laid her on the earthen floor under the Lady of Guadalupe.

"Here's a blanket to cover the baby," Dolores said, glad that the hard work was over and that she could play with the little girl too. She gave her a towel. "It will be cool tonight," she remarked. "Cover her well. The winter rains are coming."

"Sleep tight, baby," said Tomás. "And now, Mommy, I must go fishing. Good-bye." He picked up his tackle box and blew her a kiss.

Out in the street Tomás could hear other families celebrating Christmas in laughter and conversation behind their fences. Children kicked balls and played with new toys in the dusty road, and music blared from every *palapa* and casa. Above the happy sounds of Christmas Day in Loreto came the glorious song of the orioles, who were setting up their spring territories in the trees of Colonia Zaragosa. The air had warmed, and the sky shone crepe-paper blue.

"This is the day. This is the day," Tomás sang as he passed the Morélloses' casa. José was not to be seen—probably still sleeping, he thought with a smile. That was a great night for José.

He hurried on to the beach, wondering if José would start his own firecracker business with Victorio. It seemed too good to be true. All the combustibles his friend could possibly want would be his. Then Tomás wondered how the profits would be divided and if José would get his fair share.

Why am I thinking about such things? he asked himself. Is it the spirit of my father in the fishing tackle box that is making me a responsible man, thinking reasonable thoughts?

Tomás blinked his eyes, and José's problem was gone. His thoughts lightened. He was going to dive with the incredible Uncle Díaz. He was on his way to conquer a shark. He ran the last stretch to the fishermen's beach.

The green boat cast a long shadow on the water, indicating that it was two o'clock. Uncle Díaz was not there. Tomás scanned the beach for him. He saw only a young boy and girl picking up shells at the water's edge, two men sleeping under the date palm and a group of ninth-graders kicking a soccer ball around. He walked to a palm and sat down.

After a long while Tomás put on Uncle Díaz's diving mask and began to imagine the wonders the great diver had seen through it. Had Uncle Díaz looked out on the deep-living Sierra mackerel, the rare porcupine fish with its covering of movable spines or the wrecks of the conquistadors' ships?

He tried to imagine himself coming upon a black coral at ninety feet. How his lungs ached as he cut the sea jewel from its rock, and how he sucked in life-giving air when he finally shot to the surface.

Then he stabbed the whale shark. He lifted it and carried it over the sea to Griselda. Her green eyes glistened with admiration, and she laughed and called his name.

Tomás took off the mask.

The shadow of the boat had grown longer, the water a darker blue. The children were wandering homeward, and the soccer players were gone. Overhead the turkey vultures circled down toward their night roost.

Tomás looked up the street. He could see past the Morélloses' gate to the crossroads. Uncle Díaz was nowhere in sight.

He is not coming to meet me, Tomás realized.

In sadness Tomás picked up his tackle box. He would get the shark by himself. The rent for the island must be paid.

Biting his lips to quell his disappointment, he stopped at José's gate and looked in. A fire was still burning in the pit where the pig had been roasted. In the blue twilight he could see the Morellos family moving from kitchen to garden, hear José's little sisters giggling and smell the sweet odor of pork. He pushed open the gate and walked to the brick hideout. A candle was burning in the cave.

"José," he called softly. "José!"

"Tomás!" José stuck his head out of the laboratory. "What's up?"

Tomás hesitated.

"Is Uncle Díaz here?" he finally asked.

"Uncle Díaz?" José said. "I don't know where he is. He went to town after we butchered the hog. I haven't seen him since. Why?"

"I was just wondering," Tomás answered softly. José came out of the cave, brushing the dust from his Christmas pants.

"I don't have enough chemicals to even start the double-streamer rocket, never mind the black powder," he said. "I'll have to wait until Uncle López gets here."

"What about Victorio?" Tomás asked.

"Oh, I've forgotten about him. He probably didn't mean it anyway," answered José.

"I guess not," said Tomás. "I guess not. People are funny that way."

"Have You Come for Me?"

FOR fifty years Ramón had returned to his fish camp on Coronados Island the first Monday after the Christmas week. This year he did not. He put on his best clothes and his broad-rimmed sombrero, then waited for Miguel to dress. Together they walked the path to the casa gate, their faces showing no emotion. They were going to meet with the *oficiales* this morning.

Tomás walked with them as far as the government offices in the center of Loreto. When they had gone into the white stucco building with its arched windows and decorative balconies, Tomás crossed to the town park. He sat down on a bench in front of the bronze bust of the Mexican hero Benito Juárez, the pure-blooded Zapotec Indian who became president of Mexico in 1861 and again in 1867.

While Tomás waited, elbows on his knees, chin on his fists, he thought about this president. He had come from a poor Indian family but had managed to study law, defend the poor for no charge and eventually become the president of Mexico. As president he had broken up the enormous and wealthy estates of the church and other rich landholders and divided much of the land among the peasants and fishermen.

Then he had gone after the schools. The church had run them for the rich and elite; the poor had been unable to attend. Juárez had reorganized the system so that every child went to school; in fact, he had required them to attend through sixth grade. "Go to school and learn," he had said to the children of the poor. "Mexico needs you."

A good man, mused Tomás. He sure did a lot with his schooling.

Miguel came out of the government building, his sombrero askew, and crossed the busy street to find Tomás.

"We will be a long time," he said. "The line is very, very long. Go home and cheer up the women."

"All right," Tomás said, and walked worriedly back to Colonia Zaragosa, hoping Bruja would appear to comfort him. He did not.

After explaining the delay to the anxious women, Tomás flipped on Miguel's battery-run radio. When a tango played, he bowed to his grandmother, took her in his arms and danced her gracefully over the earthen floor. She smiled with pleasure while Francisca and little María clapped. Digna rang the pretty clay bell in time to the music and the Tórreses' casa was a field of music and laughter.

When the music stopped, Tomás seated his grandmother and bowed to her with a flourish. "Señora, you are a star," he said. "Now let us all drink coffee while we wait for the good news."

"You, Tomás?" his grandmother said. "You never drink coffee."

"I do now," he answered. "As of this moment."

"Next thing you know," his mother said, "you'll be asking for wine." He grinned, feeling very much in charge of the casa and liking the responsibility enormously.

The homeside family drank coffee until late in the morning and until they could drink no more.

Finally Dolores got to her feet and smoothed down the unironed skirt she had put on hastily this morning.

"Whatever happens," she said, "I will still have my work to do." She walked into the yard and turned the hose into the laundry tub. Tomás could see her throwing wood into the fire pit to heat the water in the huge tin container; then she returned to the *palapa* and gathered a basket of clothes.

"I have work to do too," said Digna. "I cannot sit around waiting for *oficiales* to determine my fate. It's already determined. I market." She counted pesos from the money box kept in the chest of drawers and went off to the *supermercado.* Francisca picked up the broom and began sweeping.

Tomás sat down on his bed and opened his father's fishing tackle box.

"Mother," he said, "what did my father catch on this bright yellow spinner with the many hooks?"

"I do not know," she answered, kneeling to sweep the dirt into the dustpan. "I only know he was a very good fisherman."

"Did he ever catch whale sharks on these hooks and spinners?"

"I do not know anything about his tackle box. He kept it on the island. When Ramón gave it to me after his death, I put it in my personal box." She straightened up. "I never looked in it until you did." Her fingers tightened on the broom handle and she glanced around. No one was within earshot, which did not happen often in the crowded, open home, and she took advantage of the privacy.

"Tomás," she said. "I may go to work."

Tomás slammed the lid of the tackle box closed and stared at her. Griselda's aunt could work, and the widow who ran the beauty parlor in Loreto could work, and even the merchants' wives—but not a fisherman's wife, and certainly not his mother.

"No, please don't do that," he said, getting up. "You don't have to. Everything will be all right very soon. The fish will come back and we'll have pesos again."

"Times are changing," Francisca said gently. "Many married women are going to work to help their families." She stepped closer to her son. "José's aunt has a lady friend who works at the *supermercado.* She likes the work, and she says the pay is good—three thousand pesos a day. She thinks she can get me a job."

"No," Tomás said with anguish in his voice. "In June I'll be out of school, and I can help Ramón and Miguel every day. That should take care of the island rent."

"José's father," Francisca went on, ignoring him, "told José's mother, who told me, that the *oficiales* want fifteen thousand pesos a month rent for the island. That's a lot of money. We cannot pay that, even with you working." Tomás was listening intently. She continued.

"The fishing is no longer good enough to pay for our needs, much less the rent. I know. I am good at figures. Everything keeps costing more and more. I must go to work, Tomás. It will be all right. I'll probably like it. I am really nothing in this family without my husband. Just another mouth to feed."

"That isn't so," Tomás said with indignation. "You are very important. You're my mother." Hurt by her words, he looked down at the tackle box and saw the whale shark swimming under the overhang. He dreamed, and put on Uncle Díaz's mask, clutched a rock and, leaping overboard, rode swiftly to the bottom. The great shark came toward him. Tomás threw his spear into its heart. Now he was gathering up hundreds of thousands of pesos—payment for the shark. Good had won.

Tomás walked close to his mother and looked into her dark eyes.

"Everything is going to be all right," he said. "I'm going to fix it."

"Of course you will," she answered with a tender smile, and went back to her sweeping.

Tomás packed his snorkel and Uncle Díaz's mask in his clothing bag together with a change of clothes and picked up his spear. He would get a ride to the island somehow. Without telling either his mother or his grandmother where he was going, he walked off.

At the crossroads he saw Ramón and Miguel coming up out of the dusty arroyo. He ran to meet them. Ramón was limping again, and the lines in his face were drawn down like tree roots.

"Is the news bad?" Tomás asked.

"Not good," Ramón answered. "We must pay fifteen thousand pesos a month in rent. And that is not the end of it. The *ofi-*

ciales want more tourists to visit the island. So—we will not be able to clean our fish there anymore. The smell of fish offends the tourists, they say. The *oficiales* also said our camp looks trashy."

"Trashy?" Tomás felt as if he had been stung by a boatload of sea nettles. He hurt all over. "How can they say that? It's beautiful. It's a castle. I love it."

"Tomás," said Ramón, "while Miguel and I talk this over at home, would you take the *ponga* out to the island and bring in the shark fins? We must sell them today."

Tomás's face brightened. He had been given a means to get to the island.

"I have some fins drying on the flat rock behind the second beach," Miguel said. "Bring them along too. With the sale of all our fins we can pay the first month's rent and hope the *oficiales* change their minds. They are always changing their minds."

"Don't worry," Tomás said earnestly. "We will pay the first rent and the second and fiftieth. I know we will." He turned and ran down the road toward the sea.

"Tomás!" It was José calling. "Where are you going?"

"Shark fishing," he answered without slowing his pace.

"Wait a minute." José ran to catch up with him. "I saw Señor Fuertes this morning when I was out looking for Uncle Díaz. He wants to talk to your family. He will drop by your casa today." Tomás hurried on. José trotted beside him.

"Are you going to go to high school, Tomás?"

"I don't know. Are you?"

"No. Last night the padre telephoned Uncle López's boss about my rocket," he said. "The boss wants me to work for him. Five thousand pesos a day, and more when I learn. When school is out, I'll take the bus to La Paz and the ferry to Topolobampo. Uncle López will meet me there. Isn't that something?"

"Won't you be lonely so far from home?"

"I am grown up. Besides, Uncle López has two sons, three daughters, a father- and mother-in-law, two aunts and an uncle living with him. It'll be just like home."

"I'll miss you, José."

"I'll mail you a rocket with double streamers."

They strode along side by side, the dust puffing up from their bare feet, their thoughts on the changes to come. When Tomás saw the *ponga,* he sprinted to the beach and threw his gear aboard. José caught up with him again.

"You said Ramón wants you to go to school. What do you

want to do?"

"Miguel and my mother want me to be a fisherman," he said, evading an answer. He checked the gas in the Evinrude.

"You should go to school, Tomás. You're real smart. You catch on to things. You could be a good teacher."

"José," Tomás said.

"What?"

"Did you find Uncle Díaz?"

"Yes."

"Where was he?" Tomás's voice was barely audible.

"He was sitting in front of the scuba-divers' shop, drunk as a bee in a wine glass. He was wearing a mask and killing sharks." José laughed and shook his head, the laugh to express his understanding, the head shake to express his pain.

Tomás nodded. He already knew the truth, but he wanted to hear it spoken. Hearing it made it real and understandable. Tomás put his shoulder to the *ponga* and pushed the boat toward the water. The tide was going out, and he had a good distance to go. José helped, shoving with his hands. A mestizo surf fisherman saw them struggling and put down his rod, and he too helped. Three more men walked up. They each grabbed a side of the *ponga* and ran it quickly into the sea.

Tomás thanked everyone, jumped in and pushed out into deep water with an oar. He waved to José and started the motor. When it hummed, Tomás swung the *ponga* around and sped seaward.

Everything is going to be just fine, he thought, giving the engine gas.

The bow lifted, and spray spread out behind the boat like wings. Tomás was flying to the red island in the green-blue sea. As he approached the white beach of Coronados, he cut off the motor and leaned over the side of the boat. The tide was relatively high, the water deep. He slipped the mask over his eyes, put the snorkel in his mouth and jumped overboard.

He grabbed the boat in terror.

The mask! he thought. It makes the water look like air. I thought I was going to fall and kill myself. He spewed brine and, hanging on to the boat for dear life, looked down again.

The floor of the sea was not the fuzzy checkerboard he was used to seeing through his uncovered eyes. It was drifts of tiny sand grains and neatly stacked walls of volcanic pebbles that the waves and currents had lifted and set down systematically. The fish were not misty jewels, but as clear as their paintings in the scuba-diving shop, and the brittle stars had bands of color on them, not misty ripples.

What a difference! he thought, still clinging to the boat as he looked around. A bull's-eye puffer was sleeping under the sand, but it was quite visible through the mask, for its fins stirred up tiny puffs of silt that outlined the body. A school of smoothtail manta rays, a small species, flapped past on their way to the reef to have the barberfish and damselfish clean them.

This is a whole new world, Tomás thought, and climbed back into the *ponga,* gassed the engine and followed the manta rays. Not far from the reef he jumped overboard again. A school of needlefish serpentined toward him. To his left the water bent, and the talons of an *águila,* the sea eagle, appeared below the surface. They closed on a needlefish. Tomás lifted his head out of the water and pushed back the mask to watch the bird. Just above the water the eagle crooked its wings into flying position and flapped across the sky, the needlefish writhing in its talons like a sea-serpent.

Quetzalcoatl, there you are in the feet of the eagle. Stay with me. The pelicans saw the eagle's success and bombed into the water. The gulls saw the pelicans eat and swam up to them to steal fish from their huge pouches.

Tomás climbed back aboard and eased the *ponga* along the reef. He was at peace with himself. The island was serene; the fish camp on the beach before him was golden and cozy.

"Trashy!" he snorted out loud. "How can they say that? It is paradise." He tilted his head and looked at the *palapa* tucked against the red rocks of the dyke and smiled at its beauty. I guess I am, and will always be, a fisherman, he thought. Grandpapa was right; time is beginning to make up my mind for me.

Suddenly Tomás devoutly wished he did not have to go back to Loreto and make up his mind. He would live in the cave on the other side of the volcano, safe from *oficiales* and the school board. He would fish for food and dive for pleasure. For companionship he would talk to the sea lions who lived on the east side of Coronados. He would—

"Dreaming again," he said, and snapped himself to attention. I'd better check on my shark, he thought. Adjusting the mask, he grabbed his spear and a stone and jumped overboard. He plunged past a school of jacks that were darting like arrows through the water, and sped toward the bottom. Starfish and anemones became more abundant the lower he went.

His old, familiar friends were as clear through the mask

as were the birds on the land—and they were as varied and beautiful.

The bumphead parrot fish was gone, but its home was occupied by a juvenile leather bass, strikingly barred with dark-and-white stripes that had been blurs to Tomás before. The fish saw him and moved into the spines of a sea anemone. The spines did not sting it to death as they did other fish, for the bass had evolved a chemical that made it immune to the anemone's poison. In its spines it was safe from enemies. A group of grazing fish came wheeling by. They frightened a school of tiny bethnic fish that recognized the group as predators and hid in the rock cracks. The leather bass saw where they hid and left the anemone. Standing on its head, it swallowed the bethnic fish like a chicken eating corn.

Señor Fuertes says I can learn about fish in school, he mused. I would really like that.

Tomás did not see the shark under the overhang and wondered if it had recovered from its wounds and returned to the open sea. Or maybe, he reasoned, it's at the far side of its circling path, out in the Shallows, and will soon be back. That's most likely. I'll go see.

Climbing back into the *ponga,* he ran it closer to the reef and dropped the anchor. With spear in hand he eased into the water and, grabbing the anchor line, pulled himself swiftly down it.

As he descended, he could clearly see for the first time the many levels of the reef dwellers. It was still almost high tide, and the society of fishes arranged themselves somewhat differently than at low tide. Near the surface swam the Mexican needlefish and the scissortail damselfish. They mingled with the burrito grunts, the halfbeaks and giant damselfish. Lower down on the rocky wall dwelled a gorgeous king angelfish, with its dark-blue body, bold white bar and bright-yellow tail. It fanned its blue fins as it grazed a sponge. Not far away, in a stony cave lined with bright coral, his mate hovered. The two were monogamous, bonded to each other for life. The female darted at Tomás, defending her life and territory. He swam closer and saw, to his amazement, a brood of juveniles swimming beneath her.

Oh, what I have been missing, he said to himself. The female takes care of her babies. I never knew that before. They were too small to see without a mask.

On down, three Moorish idols were waiting in line to be cleaned by the barberfish. They were black and white, and some of the most beautiful of the reef fishes. Their eyes and snouts were elaborately lined with black-and-brown stripes, and their dorsal fins were long arches that tapered off into delicate filaments. Tomás recalled hearing somewhere that Moorish idols were favorites of aquarium owners in the United States and that they paid outrageous prices for them. He had never thought of catching them before, but if the sharks were vanishing, perhaps he, Ramón and Miguel should harvest these beautiful fishes.

Then they would vanish like the black coral, he realized. There were no easy answers.

Now Tomás peered under the overhang. No shark, he thought in disappointment. His luck was truly bad—no ship, no Uncle Díaz, no shark.

His breath was running out, but he was pleased with his endurance. He was staying down longer. He surfaced, breathed and went down again.

A zebra moray eel darted at him from a rock crevice. Tomás pushed it away as he pulled himself down on the anchor line to the seafloor, sixteen feet below the *ponga.* A gathering of blue-spotted jawfish, with their sky-blue spots and yellow fins, hung motionless at his feet. Each jawfish was near a deep burrow it had constructed of shell fragments and pebbles. When night came, each would retire inside and build a lid over its entrance. Some of the jawfish were courting females, hanging motionless with their back fins erect. Suddenly a male did a headstand and whipped its tail back and forth until the rear end of its body turned black.

That's the mating dance Señor Fuertes told me about, Tomás thought, and went up for air. I've never seen that before.

On the next dive he dropped straight down to the sandy bottom, where the flag cabrillas and the shy spotted sand bass lived. He swam up to the sand bass. Its eye is tear shaped and mean like a dragon's eye, he observed. That's new to me. I could stay here all day. If I went on to school, I would know more about these creatures on the reef. As Tomás moved toward the sand bass to get a closer look, he put his foot in a garden of question marks. They were fish that stood upright in the sand, their long, skinny bodies swaying with the movement of the water and their necks cricked like question marks.

Wow! he thought. These are the Cortés garden eels that Uncle Díaz told me about.

A shadow fell across the eels. Tomás looked up, and his heart banged. A shark was torpedoing toward him, a scar on its belly and tail, its jaws wide open. He thought of his father.

My shark! It's a hammerhead!

Tomás shot to the surface and, grabbing the anchor line, shouting in pain, pulled himself hand over hand into the *ponga.*

"He hit me! He hit me!" Rolling to his back, he closed his eyes so he would not see blood spurting from his aching thigh. He saw his father, his unremembered face smiling at him.

"Have you come for me?" Tomás called out to him. "Do you want me with you? Did you send the shark for me?" He opened his eyes, saw no blood on his uplifted leg and sat up. A welt was rising where he had been struck, but that was all. Tomás looked over the gunwales into the sea. The hammerhead swirled in a tight circle below him.

"Why didn't you kill me?" he shouted at the fish. "Am I to be spared? Why? Why me and not my good father?" As if in answer, the enormous shark came back. The glassy black eyes on the ends of the strange head focused on the boat. The jaws opened and slammed closed on the *ponga.* Tomás's heart thundered.

"Quetzalcoatl!" he cried. "Grandpapa! Miguel! Where are you?"

Of Sharks and Men

TOMÁS hobbled to the outboard motor and started it up.

A huge hammerhead, he thought. Now what do I do? I can't go down and kill him with my spear. I'd be dead.

The pelicans and eared grebes had scooted into the shallow waters of the cove, away from the killer shark. Over the reef a tiny white Forster's tern screamed its warning cry.

"I hear what you are saying at last," he called to the birds. "Danger. Killer shark. That's what you've been telling me all along." A movement on the volcano caught his eye, and he glanced up. Two vultures had taken off from their nest near the summit and were soaring on up-tipped pinions toward him.

"No you don't!" he cried, shaking his fist at them. "I'm alive. And I'm staying alive." He shivered as he thought about the many times he had jumped off the reef without even a knife to protect himself as he sought the shark he thought was a whale shark. He ran his fingers through his hair and shook his head.

How could I be so dumb?

But I never did get a good look at him. I never did see his head. Tomás rubbed his leg. But then, even if I had, I would have seen a whale shark. I wanted to see a whale shark—the one Miguel saw coming up out of the deep. My mother's right. I do dream, and I do see what I want to see. But no more. I am fourteen now. I am more practical.

Tomás ran the *ponga* up onto the beach and jumped into the tips of the waves, where hosts of little hermit crabs were carrying their shell houses to the water to keep up with the ebbing tide.

Maybe, little crabs, he thought, maybe I should get the shark on rod and reel. The sportfishermen do; why not I? I'd be a lot safer.

Limping to the shade of the *palapa* porch, he took down Ramón's marlin fishing rod and reel and, holding it up in the light, smiled at this solution to his problem.

But first, he thought, I had better do what I was sent out here to do—get the shark fins. He took a large raffia bag and climbed the dyke to the drying arena, where he gathered up the entire batch. Then he limped up and over the dyke to Miguel's cache, in the sun above the second beach. When the fins were all collected, he looked out at the reef and thought about his shark again.

It's in poor health, he mused. It shouldn't put up too much of a fight. But it's big and it's heavy. Still, Grandpapa's line ought to hold it; it holds a two-hundred-pound marlin. But ten feet of shark? It'll weigh more than that. Maybe a rod and reel is not such a hot idea. Snap goes the line—I lose it again.

As he came down the dyke, he saw the shark nets stretched out on the sand to dry.

"Net him!" he said aloud. Of course. That's how the Tórreses always catch their sharks—with nets. What have I been thinking about? I'll set it along the reef and scare or lure the shark in. He ran to one of the nets and took hold of it to drag it to the boat.

"Phew," he said. Not this net. I'll never set this heavy thing alone. He scratched his head and, remembering the smaller bait net in back of the *palapa,* found it and dragged it to the *ponga.* It was one hundred feet long instead of three hundred, and of finer cord but still very strong. He put it in the *ponga.*

The anchors and the floats went in next; then he returned to the *palapa,* picked up a bucket and hiked off to the dump. This was the refuse pile the *oficiales* had complained about, the odoriferous spot where the Tórreses threw the remains of their fish for the birds after filleting them. Tomás filled the bucket with a stinking carcass the vultures and gulls had not finished.

Does smell, he thought, taking a breath. But it's nice. Gringos should learn to appreciate the good, rich smell of the sea. He grimaced and wrinkled his nose.

Tomás ground the bones and fins in the salt grinder to make chum, a smelly soup that draws the toothed sharks as a metal pole in an open field draws lightning.

His thigh throbbed painfully, and he pulled up his pant leg to take a look at the place the shark had hit. He was not sure whether he had been hit with its head or its tail, but certainly the shark had not hit him with its teeth, or else he would be bleeding. His thigh was swollen and already turning thunderstorm black and blue.

A souvenir from my shark, he thought proudly, and wondered if he should show it to Griselda. He thought not. She wasn't *that* modern.

Checking to see if there was anything else he needed before setting out, he picked up the boat oar, took a long, deep breath and bravely launched himself on a shark hunt.

He paddled to the reef so as not to make noise, wishing to come up on the hammerhead as quietly as possible. Next he eased down the north side. Putting on his mask, he leaned into the water and looked down. Two feet of hammerhead tail protruded from the overhang as the huge fish moved slowly forward, gasping for aerated water. Tomás could actually see the current the shark was seeking. It carried bits of debris swiftly along the bottom.

Tomás dropped one anchor and float. Starting the motor, he quietly fed out the net, making a wide semicircle around the hammerhead, then dropped the second anchor and float. The lead sinkers dragged the net to the seafloor; the buoys lifted and stretched it out. He put on the mask again and looked down to check his work.

Perfect, he thought. The net is stretched from shallow water to halfway down the reef. He kept looking.

The shark, which was now swimming wearily, reached the end of the overhang and swam out into the sea. It circled back and under the overhang again.

Tomás saw that the tail of his monster was twitching. The net and the *ponga* were making it nervous.

Suddenly it shot out, struck the boat and dived. Now Tomás was nervous. He had seen the attack with his face underwater, and he shivered. The ungainly head was devilish—a Tezcatlipoca. The huge, black eyes were as mean as the ends of a gun barrel. They relentlessly stared up, out, back and down—in every direction and all at once, the better to see and kill.

As Tomás watched, the shark turned, and light struck the millions of teeth embedded in the pores of its skin; they shone like daggers. The hammerhead wore a diabolical armor that could rip off sheets of human skin with one swipe.

No you won't, thought Tomás, and picked up the bucket of chum. He dumped it into the water on the other side of the net from the shark. Stepping back to the reef side of the boat, he watched and waited.

The tired hammerhead quivered like a hurled spear as the chemicals of fish reached its nose brain. Time passed; the shark did not come for the food.

It must be nearly dead and won't eat, Tomás concluded. I'll pull the net tighter against the reef and drive it in with an oar. Tomás motored to the farthest buoy, hooked a grappling iron in it and, with the engine, pulled it taut. It flattened against the rocks. Tomás closed down the motor and waited some distance away.

An hour passed. The tide ebbed lower, the volcano turned from red to purple. Neither one of the floats bobbed to say the shark had entangled itself. Something was wrong. Tomás looked around for an explanation. The eared grebes were diving and swimming near the net. A flock of tiny, white Forster's terns were plunging from the air into the water, catching surface fish. Three cormorants flew to the reef and sat down. They casually preened.

"This time," Tomás said to the birds, "you are telling me there is no killer shark. Where is it?" He put on the mask and was about to stick his head under to see what was the matter when he heard an outboard motor. He turned around. Zoro and Jesús were headed his way.

I sure don't want them here, he thought, starting his own motor. He met the fox and his son at the edge of the Shallows.

"Hi, Tomás." Jesús waved.

"Jesús," called Tomás, "did the *oficiales* get you yet?"

A wind skipped down from the sky and wrinkled the water.

"Not us," Zoro answered, and laughed heartily. "But I hear they got Ramón."

Tomás nodded gravely as he pulled alongside and grabbed their boat. "We have to pay rent for the island."

"Not me. I won't," Zoro shouted. "They'll never catch me. I camp in a different place each night." His teeth gleamed like spearheads behind his heavy, dark lips. He was enjoying the game of hide-and-seek.

Jesús, who was almost as keen eyed as a vulture, saw the net floats along the reef.

"Tomás," he asked, "why are you fishing so close to the rocks? You're some crazy fisherman. The evening winds are coming up. They'll dash your net on the rocks and rip it to pieces."

Like a predator that has caught the scent of prey, Zoro stepped up on the bow of his boat, tweaking the peak of his baseball cap, and studied the scene at the reef.

"You after that wounded hammerhead?" he asked.

Tomás did not answer.

"I saw it there yesterday," Zoro went on. "We've come out to get him." He scowled at Tomás's rig.

"Get that out of here," he barked. "I'm going to shoot it."

"It's my shark!" Tomás yelled, and got to his feet. "The reef is ours."

"Mexico's beaches and reefs belong to everyone," Zoro replied, pulling his fur coat over his bare chest, for the wind was suddenly blowing harder and colder.

"Not after today," Tomás said. "Things have changed. We are renting. We are paying for the right to fish here."

"The Constitution says the island waters belong to the Mexican people—all of them—rent or no rent."

Zoro picked up a rifle from the bottom of his boat.

"Jesús," he said, "line us up with the last rock on Coronados Island and the peak of El Pescador on Carmen. That will bring us in where we saw the shark yesterday."

Jesús did as he was told, taking a bearing and gassing the engine just enough to move the boat slowly on course. Still standing on the bow, Zoro took a wide stance, rifle in his hands.

"Don't!" Tomás yelled. They moved steadily and relentlessly on.

Tomás put the Evinrude in gear, feeling absolutely helpless. And then a drama began to unfold. The wind blew harder, whipping up rough surface waves that were opaque and difficult to see through. Zoro shaded his eyes and leaned closer to the water.

The wind's helping me, Tomás thought. It's supposed to be the evil spirit of Tezcatlipoca; but it sure is good right now. Stir up the sea, devil wind. Stir up the sea.

With a sudden leap Tomás was on the boat seat. He was in trouble. The waves were tossing the net toward the rocks. Ramón's valuable net was about to be torn to shreds. How can one thing be both good and bad at the same time? he wondered. Now the wind is evil.

He did not have time to work that one out. I've got to bring Grandpapa's net in right now, he thought, and turned up the gas.

Zoro was raising the gun to take aim.

Lady of Guadalupe, Tomás silently cried. Please do not let Zoro get my shark. Please do not. He closed his eyes and prayed.

When he opened them, Zoro's boat was against the net, his gun was now at his shoulder. The Lady of Guadalupe was not listening. She had more important things to do.

Please, Quetzalcoatl, he begged silently. Come down from the planet Venus. Let the forces of good win, like they do in the Christmas pageant.

Zoro put his eye to the gunsight, and Jesús headed their boat into the waves so it would not rock.

Lady of Guadalupe, Quetzalcoatl, whoever is out there: Why are you doing this to me? Is it because I cannot make up my mind? Is it because I want to be a student one minute and a fisherman the next? I cannot help it. I do not know which is the good. Show me what to do.

Tomás looked over his hands, which were pressed together in prayer. The wind had suddenly died, and the waves were smooth and glassy. Zoro could see.

Tomás waited for the shot. It did not come. Something had changed Zoro's mind.

"Jesús," Zoro yelled. "Go toward the buoy. The net is dragging on the bottom. I can't see the shark."

Suddenly Tomás knew what was happening—the shark was in his net. And Zoro was going to shoot and claim it as his.

No, Quetzalcoatl, he prayed. You can't let that happen. Zoro can't take a shark from another fisherman's net. The waters might belong to all Mexicans, but the net belongs to Ramón. No fisherman is so evil as to take fish from another fisherman's net.

Quetzalcoatl, stop him.

Tomás came in closer, trying to wedge his *ponga* between Zoro and the net.

He backed up; Zoro had lifted his gun again. Evil was going to win.

What can I do to stop him? Tomás remembered that the actors in the pageant gave gifts to the saints to be assured that the forces of good won out.

I have nothing to give, he thought, except my fishing tackle box.

But that is materialistic. The forces of good cannot come down and get it. Not even my father comes back. I have seen the dogs carry off the food we leave for him.

I must give something of me—something important. He thought. I'll make a decision. That's what I'll give—my decision.

Zoro had dropped to his knees and was pointing the gun straight down. He clicked off the safety.

Lady of Guadalupe, Quetzalcoatl, all the forces of good, Tomás prayed in desperation. If you send Zoro away, if you let me catch my shark, I will—I will become a fisherman for the rest of my life. If you let me catch my shark, I will do that. I will be a fisherman.

The shot rang out.

Tomás stopped praying. A wind struck him across the back. He turned and looked back. Clouds filled the western sky. Black and purple, they charged down the mountains like angry bulls. They were the cold wind clouds from the Pacific Ocean racing toward the hot winds from the Mexican mainland, and they would collide as they did every year at this time and explode into wild and vicious storms.

Tomás was both glad and not glad to see them. They meant rain for the parched desert, but they meant Ramón's net would be torn. The net was his concern. He steered toward it and, snagging it with a grappling iron, began to bring it, hand over hand, into the *ponga.*

Another shot rang out.

Sharks die slowly, Tomás thought.

The boats bumped together.

Zoro was grinning.

"It's mine," he said. "I shot it. That takes precedence over whose net it's in." Tomás was still pulling the net aboard. Leaning far out over the gunwales, he grabbed the mesh, leaned back and hauled. Coming to the surface, entangled in the net, was the shark. Its skin teeth flashed iridescent green-blue. The fish was magnificent.

Tomás put the motor in reverse and backed away. He had his shark.

"What are you doing?" Zoro snarled.

Tomás pulled the shark along behind him.

"It's mine!" Zoro shouted. "I shot it!"

The excited Tomás pulled in one anchor and buoy. He was on his way home with his shark.

"Jesús!" Zoro yelled. "Get that shark!"

Jesús grabbed a grappling iron and snagged the net. With all his strength he pulled net and shark toward his boat. Tomás snapped on Uncle Díaz's mask and jumped in, clothes and all.

Pulling himself along the net until he was just above the shark, he went under to cut away Jesús's grappling iron and saw the eye of the shark. It was milky. The shark was dead.

Zoro did kill him, he thought. The forces of evil had won. Tomás surfaced, held on to the net and wished he could cry. He could not, for he could not give up. He grabbed the grappling iron and pulled it out of Jesús's hand.

"Get out of the way!" Zoro shouted and picked up another iron. He raised it above his head and Tomás quickly swam out of the way. Pulling the net and shark with him, he headed for the reef.

"Come back here!" Zoro roared. A wave picked Tomás up and carried him above the rocks and then deposited him upon them. With him came the shark in the net. The wave ran out and left them high and dry. Tomás looked down at the hammerhead. There were no bullet wounds. The shark had died in the net.

Jesús brought their *ponga* up to the reef.

"Give me that shark!" Zoro yelled.

"It's mine!" Tomás shouted back. "It drowned in the net. There is no bullet hole."

Zoro raised the grappling iron again.

"Tomás, get the devil out of here," the fox snapped. "No pesky kid is going to take this shark from me."

A huge wave rolled in. Now Ramón's boat was in danger of crashing on the reef, and Tomás ran a few steps to hold it off. Zoro reached out with his grappling iron and struck the hammerhead. He pulled it toward him.

A strong push kept the *ponga* from the reef, and Tomás went back to the net to find that Zoro had his grappling iron in the shark's tail. A wave rolled in and lifted the shark, so Zoro was able to pull it alongside his boat. Helpless, Tomás watched him drag his shark from the net. Then he gasped. Zoro's grappling hook was in a deep wound—no doubt the one Tomás had made with the hook and line before Christmas. As Tomás watched, the grappling iron slid down the tear—and out. The shark settled back into the net.

Tomás had another chance. Grabbing the net with both hands, he stood up and, swinging it over his shoulder, pulled like a donkey as he walked up the reef. In spite of the crashing waves, he made progress, but the progress was more to irritate Zoro than to win. He could not fight the two men any longer.

"Tomás!" It was Miguel's voice!

He turned around. Like a miracle, Miguel had arrived out of nowhere. He was standing in the little *ponga* beside Zoro, as fresh and handsome as if he had just dropped from the stars.

"Miguel!" Tomás cried out. "This is our shark. Help me."

"What's the story here, Zoro?" Miguel asked, putting his foot on the gunwale of his boat. "This shark is in our net."

"I shot it," Zoro answered, but his voice was not convincing. Face to face with Miguel he had lost his bravado.

"I wouldn't try to take it if I were you, Zoro," Miguel said, looking him straight in the eye.

"I was just trying to help the boy," Zoro said, oozing deceit and uncovering the pointed tips of his teeth when he forced a smile. "But of course now that you're here, he won't need me."

"No, he won't need you. You are free to leave," said Miguel, playing the game. "We thank you very much for your help."

Zoro did not move. Miguel did not move. Presently the fox grinned and dropped his grappling iron.

"Let's go, Jesús," he said. "Tomás doesn't need us."

"So he doesn't," said Jesús, and sat down at the helm. When Jesús had his engine in gear, Miguel removed his foot, but he did not take his eyes off the pair until they were far out in the Shallows; then he turned to Tomás.

"I'll get the other float and anchor," he called. "Take your end of the net and get back in the *ponga.* I'll move out and we'll straighten out the net.

"We'll drag the shark into the cove in the net. What a catch, Tomás! He's a beauty."

On a big swell Tomás jumped into the water and swam to the *ponga* and got in.

"Okay, Tomás," Miguel called. "I'll head for the far side of the cove, you come straight in. That way we'll keep the net bowed so we don't lose the monster."

In the shallow water near the beach the huge hammerhead rose above the surface in all its majesty. Tomás stared in disbelief. It was even bigger than the whale shark of his dreams.

"Olé!" he said, his voice full of pride.

"Gun her and we'll both run up on the sand," Miguel called. "One, two, three, go!"

The sand squealed as the two boats hit the beach and jerked to a stop. The pelicans that had been sitting on the water saw the shark and took off. The grebes, however, knowing it was dead, scooted fearlessly around the huge body, snatching at the little fish that were being stirred up in the commotion.

"Grab your net anchor, Tomás," Miguel said, "and I'll take mine. We'll run them as far up the beach as we can." Tomás followed his orders, then came back.

"Now grab the net and pull when the next big wave comes in." Tomás took a good grip.

"Haul away! Haul away!"

They dug their feet into the sand, bent over and struggled up the beach. The big wave crested and rode up the sand. It picked up the heavy shark and easily carried it a distance before dropping it.

"Tezcatlipoca has sent us the wind and the waves for a winch," Miguel called, and laughed at the wonder of it. "He's a good guy now."

With the Sea of Cortez as an ally, the two fishermen of Loreto brought the gigantic hammerhead far up the beach.

"Lash a line around the head, Tomás," Miguel called. "I'll get the tail. We'll tie the monster to the rocks behind the dune. We'll have to keep pulling it higher and higher all night as the tide comes in. We need this shark."

When, at last, the hammerhead was secured and Miguel had tested the lines, he turned his attention to the storm.

"This is going to be a bad one," he said to Tomás. "We'd better anchor the boats out. They'll get battered on the beach if we don't." He watched the sky and felt the ferocity of the wind.

"We'll be up all night," he said, "keeping the sea from our shark." But he was smiling happily.

"We may not get home tomorrow," Tomás said, "if this keeps up."

"That's for sure," Miguel answered. "But not only because of the storm. That's a big shark to butcher."

"Butcher?" Tomás said. "Are we going to butcher it?"

"What do you think?" Miguel said, chuckling. "That you're going to carry it home above your head?"

"Something like that," Tomás answered, and walked over to his shark. It would be butchered—his shark was just another day's work. Tomás closed his eyes to dream of his victorious return home with the shark. He saw nothing but the fillet knife flying over the magnificent body, cutting it into small pieces for the market.

The shark trembled. The huge jaws opened, and Tomás walked closer, to look into the most vicious mouth he had ever seen. He got down on his hands and knees. The six rows of sharp teeth lay one on top of the other, pointing back toward the gullet from which nothing returned. Tomás was mesmerized. This was the demon who had taken his father. He could not move away from it. The jaws opened wider.

And Tomás spun head over heels across the sand, Miguel's iron hands imprinted on his ribs. The jaws had slammed shut, but not on the son of Ramón Jr.

"What kind of a shark fisherman are you?" Miguel roared at him. "You of all people know better than that."

Tomás stared at the shark.

"Maybe you had better go to school," his uncle said, and walked off.

Pebbles

TOMÁS fell asleep without eating; nor did he dream. After sundown the wind blew harder, tossing the waves high up the beach and rattling the limbs of the elephant trees. From time to time Miguel went out into the night and, straining to stand against the gale, winched the shark above the rising tide.

Around midnight the rain fell. Torrents emptied on the desert, sea and island. The dry, hard land, which could not absorb the water fast enough, sent it cascading down the volcano, over rocks, into pools and out again. The arroyo filled and roared like a mountain of bees.

The long-parched plants responded to the deluge, thirstily lifting the winter rain up their stems cell by cell. The trunks of the cholla and organ pipe cacti expanded. The leaf buds on ocotillo began to grow as the water flowed upward into twig and limb. The surplus was stored in reservoirs as the plants miraculously planned ahead for another drought.

Miguel awakened Tomás about midnight.

"I'm worried about the shark," he said. "The sea is very rough and high." Tomás rolled to his feet and followed Miguel into the storm. The waves were pounding the huge fish and straining the lines that held it. Using the lifting power of the waves and ignoring the stinging rain, the two managed to pull it up higher on the beach.

"And now the boats," said Miguel, splashing into the sea. He and Tomás waded into the waves until they could see the bucking, tossing *pongas*. They were riding the tumultuous sea like wood chips, as the tough little boats were designed to do.

Shivering with cold, Tomás and Miguel dashed back to the snug sleeping *palapa*. His hands shaking, Miguel laid a few dry sticks near the door and lit a fire. The *palapa* brightened and warmed. Tomás put on a dry shirt, huddled close to the flames and listened to the rain pound the palm-thatch roof.

"Not a drop is coming through," he said, shaking his head in the wonder of it. "It's amazing that a tree can give us a waterproof shingle."

"Ramón says the thatch palm is the greatest gift God ever gave to the fishermen," Miguel said. "We make it into walls and ceilings and fences and clothes and brooms and dishes and beds."

"And toothpicks and forks and fish nets and sleeping mats," Tomás went on. "It does seem like our best friend." The wind hit the palm-leaf home and it shuddered, leaned, then quickly recovered, as if to prove Tomás's words.

When he was well warmed, he pulled a blanket over himself and lay down. The rain thundered on and on, the arroyo hummed and plant parts popped and crackled as they grew. The fresh odor of wetted earth filled his nostrils, and he dropped off to sleep.

In the morning the rain was still torrential. Miguel rekindled the fire and pounded tortillas into shape. By the time he and Tomás had eaten, the storm had begun to abate. The drumming was replaced by pattering, the pattering by dripping. Miguel and Tomás sat in the doorway, drinking coffee and watching the rain ease up.

"Miguel," Tomás said after a time, "what did you and Grandpapa decide to do when you and he went home and talked? Is everything all right?" Miguel stirred the fire.

"Ramón will not pay rent," Miguel answered softly. Tomás blinked in surprise and sat straight up.

"What will the *oficiales* do if he doesn't pay the rent?" he asked. "Will they put us in jail?"

"We won't fish."

Tomás was not sure he had heard correctly.

"We won't fish?" He put down his coffee cup.

"That is correct."

"What will we do?" Tomás felt a numbness come over him. Fishing to his family was as essential as the sun. It must be. "We won't fish?" he repeated fearfully, and saw the sun fall from the sky. He tried to think of something to say but could not find the words to mouth. Holding his head, he stared out at the rain—and remembered his Christmas gift to his grandfather.

"Miguel," he said at last, "you and Grandpapa can go on fishing. I caught the shark so we could pay the rent. It will take care of it for many months. And then I'll catch another."

"It's not just the rent, Tomás," Miguel said, his voice low and even. "The fish are disappearing. We work and work and get very few pesos. And Ramón is not well. His legs bother him a lot.

"And that is not all—the real reason, Tomás," Miguel went on quietly, "is that he will not pay the bribes he would have to pay to stay on the island. He would rather not fish."

Tomás sat tall. He saw a volcano erupting in the center of his beloved family. It was spewing everyone's life into the sky—his mother's, his grandmother's and little María's, as well as Miguel's and Ramón's and his own. The Tórreses' *ponga* would not go to sea again. The Evinrude would not roar. The island, the volcano, the birds and the fish-adorned reef were all being swallowed up in the volcanic fire and smoke.

"Oh, no, Miguel!" Tomás cried. "No. You and I can fish with rod and reel from the *ponga.* Marlin and tuna bring good prices."

A wind wailed over the *palapa* and screamed off through the cacti. It *rattattoo*ed the mesquite limbs and bent the elephant trees. Miguel did not answer.

"I worked well with you when we landed the shark, didn't I? We can do that every day. I am pretty good at rod-and-reel fishing. And I really can spear fish."

Miguel rubbed his cold hands together and held them over the fire, as if the rubbing would produce the miracle needed to help them. When the chill was gone, he folded his arms and stuck his hands into his warm armpits.

"Your teacher, Señor Fuertes," he said, "came to the casa yesterday. He talked a long time about you. There's a future for you. He and Ramón think you should go to school."

"No," said Tomás. "No, I can't."

"Señor Fuertes said you could work in the new laboratory in the government high school. He said you knew a lot about the reefs and fish, and someday you could be very helpful to the fishermen."

Tomás took a deep breath. The words of his teacher set him to dreaming again. He was sailing to new worlds with Charles Darwin. He was in a laboratory with Madame Curie. He was diving deep with Uncle Díaz to study the fish of the Sea of Cortez—and he yearned for this.

A flash of lightning seemed to rip open a cloud, and the thunder boomed ferociously. Tomás crossed himself and looked up at the sky.

"I can't do it."

"Why not, Tomás?"

"Who will earn the money for the family?"

"I will work for Victorio. I will take the gringos out to fish. He will be glad to have me. He is always glad to keep another commercial fisherman off the water. More fish for his clients."

"No, Miguel," Tomás said. "I'm not going on to school. You and I will fish. We will take care of the family."

"Ramón wants you to go to school. Life is changing in Loreto. The Tórreses must change too. Like the plants and animals on this earth, we change or die. He asked me to tell you that you must be the one to go to school and help us all."

"I can't," said Tomás.

"Why not?" Miguel asked. "Why are you saying this?"

"I prayed for help."

"We all pray for help. I prayed to let Ramón live out his life on the island. See what good it does."

"My prayer was answered."

"That's good. You should be happy."

"I made a bargain."

"With the devil?"

"It seems like it. I promised to become a fisherman if I could catch this shark."

"I see," said Miguel, shaking his head. "Yes, that does make a difference." Miguel's shoulders slumped; he understood the seriousness of making a promise to the gods and saints.

The fire sent up a white coil of smoke and went out.

"You should not have done that."

"But I did."

Tomás stared up at the shipless volcano. Miguel lowered his head and traced a feathered serpent in the sand.

"I must be a fisherman," Tomás said. "Together we can do it. Will you help me?"

Miguel wiped out the serpent. "No. I can't." His voice was soft and low. "I saw Victorio before I came out here. He hired me."

"Then I'll fish alone," Tomás said, frightened but determined.

Miguel traced another serpent in the sand.

"Tomás, your decision is right. I am glad you made it. I became a fisherman when I was your age, and I've never regretted it. It's a good life."

"I know it," replied Tomás. He put his chin in his hands and looked out on the blue, green and violet sea.

"The rain is over," Miguel said after a while. "We have a lot of work before us."

Tomás stepped briskly into the clean, fresh air. The egret was back from the peninsula of Baja, where it had retreated during the storm; the pelicans were diving for fish, the vultures soaring.

Tomás untied the shark and sharpened his knife.

"Tomás?"

"Yes."

"Want to go play with the sea lions tomorrow if our work is done?"

"Sure, Miguel."

"I have a friend among them that I want you to meet. She can balance a ball on her nose. She rollicks and plays. Want to see her?"

"Sure, Miguel."

A dark wind cloud swept in from the sea and covered the volcano. Tomás watched it with apprehension, for it looked like a huge, dark bull. Its eyes were wind holes. A long tongue coiled out of its mouth.

"Tezcatlipoca," he said, "I've made my decision. Go away. No more deals."

Tomás went back to his shark. It was more than ten feet long, silvery and sleek. The pointed teeth that grew out of the skin pores gleamed in the sunlight, and the hammerhead shone like an armory of swords. The jaws were still, the eyes milky white, the nostrils closed.

Now even your jaws are dead, Tomás thought, and, taking a grip, attempted to turn the shark over.

"Miguel," he called. "I can't even budge this thing. Once I planned to carry it over my head into the plaza. How could I have ever thought I could do that?"

"You were young," answered Miguel. Tomás thought about that.

"Miguel?"

"Yes."

"Did you know there is no golden ship on the top of the volcano?"

"Yes," he answered softly. "I climbed it when I was fourteen."

Miguel smiled sadly and, getting down on his knees to begin the butchering, instead rocked back on his heels.

"But it was a beautiful ship, wasn't it?"

"I wouldn't have missed it for anything," Tomás said as he walked the length of the shark, from its head to its tail and back again. He paused to count the gill slits—five on each side. He put his finger into the spiracle, an external opening in the windpipe that is part of the primitive breathing apparatus of the shark. He traced the hearing organs with his finger, then the lateral lines down each side. Finally he stood before the head and, lifting the upper jaw, propped it open with driftwood.

A shark is really mysterious, he said to himself. Maybe my son will go to school and find out how they came to be.

Tomás gave a last honing to his fish knife and dropped to his knees beside Miguel to help him remove the fins and the tough, valuable skin. They worked well together, sensing each other's movements and intentions without wasting words. In a few moments they were joined by the gulls and pelicans, who cried for tidbits—and got them.

It was well into the afternoon before the shark was gutted, boned and filleted. Miguel cut the jaw from the head and dragged it to Tomás.

"For you," he said. "Clean it and put it in the sun to dry. It will remind you of the days when the Sea of Cortez was the greatest fishing grounds in the world."

Tomás towed the enormous jaws to the dyke and, taking out his knife, began to patiently clean them. It was almost nightfall before he asked Miguel to help him carry the jaws to the drying arena behind the *palapa.* There he propped the soft white cartilage wide open with sticks and stepped back to admire it. It stood three feet tall and spread four feet wide. The five-inch, saw-edged teeth were pearly white.

Before daylight Miguel began loading the boats with rods and reels and pans.

"What are you doing?" Tomás asked.

"Packing up everything. We must be off the island today. We'll be fined if we don't leave."

"You mean this home is no longer ours?"

"That's what I mean. Get your clothes, your shells—everything."

Tomás watched Miguel's grim face as he picked up a mat and carried it to the boat. He joined him, moving like a robot as he stowed chairs and blankets, water jugs and gasoline cans. He helped Miguel load the heavy shark nets and the three enormous bags of salted hammerhead shark meat—all that remained of Tomás's dream. He picked up a piece and laughed at the little boy who thought he was going to carry the shark whole into the plaza while the mission bells rang.

At noon Miguel cooked two large shark steaks while Tomás made the tortillas. They carried their food to the top of the dyke, sat down and looked out over the sapphire-blue water and the rain-washed Baja mountains. *Aguila,* the sea eagle, flew overhead, carrying a stick as a present for his mate.

"At least he doesn't have to move," Tomás said.

"Wait until the *oficiales* find out he's not paying rent," said Miguel. "Then he'll be moved too." Tomás looked at his uncle and lapsed into grief so deep it pained his throat.

After a silence Miguel wiped his mustache and stood up. "Now for the treat," he said, forcing a grin. "It's time to show you my sea lion, Tomás. Bring your mask."

They took off in the little *ponga,* for it was not burdened with as many possessions. Tomás was in the helm, Miguel in the bow. They sped out of the cove, then northward along the island shore. The air was fresh, and the shoulders of the volcano were changing from red to green before their eyes as millions of well-watered leaves popped open. Tomás watched the birds soaring and diving and smiled. The life of a fisherman was a good one. He was going to be happy.

It was almost two P.M.; the sportfishermen were long gone, and the sea belonged to Tomás, Miguel, the fish and the birds. Suddenly, as if it were coming from some other person inside him, he called on the Lady of Guadalupe and Quetzalcoatl again.

Please don't let me be sorry, he said silently.

At the north end of the island he steered the boat around a sculpture garden of huge, sea-carved rocks. One stood alone like a fluted castle, another had been hammered by the water into the likeness of an old man and his dog. Still others were birds and dragons. Tomás thought these massive images were the gods that the creatures of the Sea of Cortez worshipped. If so, he thought, they were nice ones that did not ask for promises and sacrifices.

He made a tight turn around the old man and the dog, sending spray into the air, then straightened his course and sped past the stony castle. On top of this the sea eagles lived. The male and the female were standing on their stick nest, looking out over their vast kingdom—ten square miles of gorgeous blue sea.

"Aren't they a noble pair?" Tomás pointed to the regal birds perched two hundred feet above the sea. Miguel did not answer; he was gauging the distance to the rocky shore.

"Pull in by the black wall, Tomás." Miguel indicated a sixty-foot-high cliff of folded lava that had solidified in the sea and been worn smooth as steel by a hundred thousand years of waves. On the dark rocks at its base lounged a herd of fourteen sea lions. Five were huge bulls, each weighing almost five hundred pounds. The females were somewhat smaller, but very large animals nevertheless. Small external ears lay tight against their pointed heads. Long, stiff whiskers stood out from their noses. Their hind feet bent forward as they sat, another characteristic that distinguished them from their cousins, the seals, whose feet stretch out behind them.

"I would like to know why mammals that have to breathe air go live in the sea," Tomás said. "Someone must know, and I would like to find him and ask that question."

When Tomás steered the *ponga* toward the herd, the sea lions emitted low, plaintive howls. As the boat drew nearer, they became agitated, and their voices changed to the sound of geese honking and dogs barking.

The boat touched the rocks. The largest bull, whose head was held high, pushed on his front flippers and rose to his full height. He honked at Miguel and Tomás, twisting his head up and to the right; then he flopped into the sea. Five other members of the herd followed him. After a minute or so they surfaced and looked at the fishermen, one of whom, Miguel, was staring at the shore.

"Come here, Pebbles," he called to a sea lion still lounging on the rocks. He held up a piece of shark meat. "Come, play with me."

Sea swells rose, carried the boat up the wall, then down again. Pebbles, a youngster of the year, born only last May, lifted her head from her bed of dark-green seaweed and watched Miguel with large, soft eyes. She moved toward him. A chorus line of Sally Lightfoot crabs danced away from her as swiftly and silently as bird shadows.

"Come, Pebbles." The young sea lion sniffed. Her whiskers twisted as she picked up the odor of fish. Two more seals dove into the sea, spiraled to the surface and grinned at the fishermen.

Miguel took off his shirt and pants, put on the mask and slipped into the dark deep water, holding a piece of shark meat in one hand.

"Toss the ball when I tell you to, Tomás. It's under the seat." Miguel breaststroked quietly toward the rookery. The bulls honked. Pebbles looked from Miguel to her kind, then back to Miguel. She honked to him, pushed with her hind feet and, sliding over the rocks, splashed into the sea. She came up six inches from Miguel's face.

"Good, girl," he said, and fed her the fish.

Miguel dove. Pebbles dove. Tomás stood up on the seat to see deeper into the clear water. Miguel and the young seal rolled and tumbled like terns on the wing.

Miguel popped up for air.

"Throw me the ball!" he called. Tomás gave it a toss, and Miguel caught it as Pebbles lifted herself until most of her long, sleek body was out of water. She honked. Miguel threw the ball to her. Miraculously she caught it on her nose and, balancing it with her whiskers, swam in circles. With a honk she tossed it back to Miguel. He caught it and swam to the boat.

"Want to play, Tomás?" Miguel called. Tomás tied the boat to a rock, slipped out of his clothes and dived in. Miguel tossed him the ball. He tossed it to Pebbles. She caught it, balanced and spun it with her long whiskers and climbed up onto the rocks. She flipped it back to Miguel.

"Here, Tomás," Miguel said, handing him the mask. "Put this on. See the most beautiful show of all."

Treading water, Tomás pulled on Uncle Díaz's mask while Miguel lured Pebbles into the water again. He dove. She dove. Tomás dove.

The underwater world at the black cliff was a sea theater where every colorful coral and brilliant reef fish of the central Baja coast performed. Against a curtain of bright coral fans and gold, blue, green, purple and orange fish swam Miguel and Pebbles side by side. He stroked her nose, she rolled over. He stroked her belly, she did a back dive and twirled into a playful dance. Rolling and spinning, she sped down into the darkness, then up again like a silver fishing spinner, outlined as she was in bubbles. She burst out of the water, dove in, then out. Miguel and Tomás watched until they had to come up for air.

When Miguel swam to the boat for more fish, Pebbles climbed in beside him, honking and talking. After she had eaten, she back-flipped into the sea and, snapping up the ball again, returned to the rocks. She tossed it to Miguel, who was almost fifty feet away; then she lay down.

"That's the end of the show," said Miguel. "Did you like it?"

"Oh, yes," Tomás said. "A fisherman's life is very special. Who else can play with a sea lion?"

They spoke no more until they were around the point of sculptured rocks.

"Who is she?" Tomás asked, leaning toward Miguel.

"I met her a week ago," he answered. "She wanted to play. I didn't teach her. What do you think about my charging gringos to bring them out here to see her perform? I could make quite a bit of money."

"No, Miguel," Tomás said sharply. "Don't do that to her. She will disappear like the sharks and fish."

Miguel ran his fingers through his hair.

"I know," he said. "That's how I figured it. You and I will keep her for ourselves."

As they entered the cove, Tomás was humming. He had never seen anything as beautiful as Pebbles, and she was not even a dream. She was real.

The Teacher

THE vultures of Colonia Zaragosa were coming home to roost when Tomás and Miguel unloaded the boats and carried their gear to Ramón's casa. At nightfall they went back for the last net. Tomás shouldered one end of it, Miguel the other. Under this burden they walked up the street. People stopped what they were doing and turned to watch. No one came forward to cheer this pageant. The finest shark fishermen in Loreto were hanging up their nets.

Uncle Díaz was sitting beside José's gate as they came by. He got to his feet and, blinking, reached out and touched Tomás's arm.

"Tomás," he said. "Is that you? I can go diving tomorrow."

"Thanks, Uncle Díaz. But I won't be going out." Uncle Díaz smiled sadly, and sat down.

At the sound of Tomás's voice José ran out of his casa gate.

"You aren't really giving up?" he asked. Tomás nodded.

"I'm glad I'm going away," José grieved, and helped Uncle Díaz to his feet.

And then it was night—the sudden night of the tropics that comes down like a triumphant theater curtain.

The streetlights failed to come on this night, and Tomás and Miguel walked in darkness. Tomás was grateful. From this moment on he was different. He was a fisherman helping to support his family, and he wanted to think about it with no eyes upon him.

In darkness Miguel and Tomás closed their gate behind them.

"Grandpapa," Tomás called, putting down his end of the net and running to the patio, where Ramón sat on his chair, looking old and tired. "I got a shark. I got a ten-foot hammerhead."

Ramón pulled up a chair for him.

"Tell me about it," he said. "Tell us all," he added, beckoning to Dolores, Francisca and Digna. María picked up her doll and sat down to listen too.

When the tale was told, each one hugged him, and Tomás realized that this was what he should have been dreaming of all along—not a gala affair in the plaza, not bells and padres praising him, but the love of the people inside the Tórreses' casa fences.

"What a fine end to your fishing career," Ramón said.

"It is not the end," Tomás said. "It is the beginning of my fishing career."

"We want you to go to school, Tomás," Francisca said. "We can all manage. I have a job washing dishes at the Café Olé." She was smiling brightly as she looked forward to being of help to her family.

Tomás glanced from face to face. They really did want him to go to school. Maybe he should. There was so much to know. His skin prickled from the thought. The Lady of Guadalupe smiled accusingly from the wall.

"I'm a fisherman, Mama," he said, too quickly and too forcibly. "A fisherman like my father."

No sooner had he spoken than he felt as if he were being ripped apart from head to toe. Juan Fuertes was pulling one arm, the Lady of Guadalupe was on the other. The result was a dull throbbing pain in his heart. He turned to Dolores to change the subject.

"I'm starving, Grandmama," he said. "Are there any burritos?"

In the blue light before sunrise Tomás walked with Miguel to Victorio's. His uncle was not smiling. For the first time in his life he was reporting to work like a bank clerk or a post office employee. He was dressed neatly, his hair combed close to his head, and although he appeared calm, he was nervously biting his lip and glancing out at Coronados Island. Working for a boss would not be easy for Miguel. He had always worked with Ramón. Tomás felt his mood very keenly. This was a sad journey.

At Victorio's hacienda Tomás told Miguel he was going to wait until Griselda came outdoors. Miguel did not wink or tease him; he simply nodded and walked on toward the sportfishing beach.

It was almost an hour before Griselda came down the casa steps and crossed the yard to the gate.

"Tomás," she said and smiled in surprise. "What are you doing here?"

Tomás hesitated, then took courage.

"Once you said to me that if I ever wanted a job with Victorio, you could get me one. Is that still true?"

"Of course," she answered. "But you are not going to fish, are you? Señor Fuertes said your grandpapa and your mother want you to go to high school."

"Can you get me the job, Griselda?"

"Yes, I can," she said flatly, staring with disbelief and not a little contempt. "I'll speak to him tonight." She brushed past him a few steps then, turning around, faced him with her hands on her hips. "I thought you were going places, Tomás Torres," she said. "This is really dumb." She spun on her heel and walked off. A curtain had been dropped between them.

Tomás was sorry; he liked her. Turning abruptly, he ran to the shore road, hoping to find a bird or a big glorious whale to watch. He looked across the water to Coronados Island. His paradise was more beautiful than ever, iron red on a silver sea. He had made a good decision.

A sudden image of Juan Fuertes passed through his mind and he felt a disturbing unhappiness until a cloud cast a fluttering shadow on the island. The island was beckoning to him to come fish the blue, blue sea.

"I'll be a good guide," he said aloud to the water and the island. "And I'll earn pesos instead of Ramón." He started back to town.

He would go tell Señor Fuertes.

Tomás found him in the science lab, seated before a stack of papers, his fingers buried in his short, black hair. Juan Fuertes was young for a teacher. He was only two years out of college, and so he wore a trim beard and mustache to give his boyish face a more adult look. He need not have bothered to grow it as far as his students were concerned. He was a teacher and teachers were ageless.

"Señor?" Juan Fuertes looked up.

"Tomás," he said eagerly and smiled. "I presume you are bringing good news."

Tomás did not answer. He squared himself before the teacher and pressed his arms to his side.

"I am not going to high school." He swallowed hard. "I will be a fisherman."

"Why is that, Tomás?"

Rapidly Tomás told Juan Fuertes the story of his shark and his bargain. When he was done, the teacher pushed back his chair until his arms were stretched to their full length. He looked across the papers right into Tomás's eyes.

"I am a teacher," he began. "It's really a misleading title. A person can't teach another person anything. One teaches himself. What a teacher can do, however, is to lead a person to think."

Tomás stood perfectly still.

"I want you to tell me the story again, Tomás, and really think about it this time. After all, any young man who can figure out why the pelican has three different colors and that the damsel fish is a farmer and weeds its garden should look a little closer at his own story. Now begin again."

"Miguel saw a whale shark," Tomás spoke slowly. "It came out of the deep sea and swam to the overhang of the Coronados reef. Knowing a whale shark is not a killer, I thought I would spear it all by myself and become a hero." He smiled sheepishly.

"All right. What else?"

"What do you mean?"

"About your decision to go to school or to fish."

"I wanted someone to make that decision for me."

"So?"

"Nobody did for a long time. Then Miguel told me to be a fisherman."

"And?"

"When the *oficiales* routed us off the island, Grandpapa told me to go to school. Miguel said, 'fish'."

"And?"

"Then a lot of things happened. I misidentified the shark—I should never have done that. I know a hammerhead, even a shy one. I nearly wrecked Grandpapa's *ponga* and net—I never should have let them get so close to the reef in a wind. I nearly got killed by a shark—I knew better than to get so close."

"And what do those facts say to you?"

"That I am not a very good fisherman." Tomás dropped his gaze to the floor.

"Is that true?"

Tomás grinned.

"Think harder."

"Well." He spoke softly, searching the wind, waves, shark and religion for a thought of a different dimension and color.

"Deep down inside me I wanted to mess up."

"Why?"

"Messing up was a decision of a sort. Everyone would know I would not make a good fisherman."

Juan Fuertes waited.

"No," Tomás said carefully. "That's not quite right. I wanted to help Ramón. I wanted that shark—so much that I bargained with the heavens."

Juan Fuertes did not speak.

"Then I saw how unreal bargaining was." He stepped closer to the desk. "The wind on the reef made *that* clear."

Juan Fuertes looked at him—waiting.

Tomás went on selecting each word carefully. "When I was out in the rising storm, I saw that the wind is not just evil as I was taught. It has many faces."

Juan Fuertes leaned closer.

"And?"

"It can be good. It can be evil, helpful, furious. It is nature."

"And?"

"You can't bargain with that."

"So what did you really want, Tomás?"

"The shark."

"What did you want, really?"

"A decision."

"And?"

"I got one. I'll stick with it."

"Tell me about the wind again, Tomás."

He knitted his brows and stared at the teacher.

"It has many faces."

Juan Fuertes folded his hands on the desk.

Tomás shifted his weight from one foot to the other.

Juan Fuertes remained silent.

Tomás climbed the volcano again, he saw the real people in the pageant again, and Uncle Díaz asleep under a tree. There were other ways to look at things.

His eyes widened.

"Hey," he said suddenly. "A fisherman is like the wind. He also has many faces; and one of them is the face of a student of the sea."

"A marine biologist," said the teacher, and, smiling broadly, opened his desk drawer and took out an official paper. He held it up. Tomás saw an application to high school.

"May I?" Juan Fuertes asked, picking up a pen to fill in the blanks.

"Yes," said Tomás, his voice trembling slightly.

As the teacher wrote down his name, Tomás saw endless waves of glittering fish welling up from the clear green waters of the Sea of Cortez. They skimmed along the reefs, sparkled in the sunlight, multiplied and grew. And all the while, he noticed, the mission bells rang and rang.

Connected Readings

Plumed Serpent in Tula

Cal Roy

"Plumed Serpent in Tula" is a myth from the Aztecs, a Native Mexican tribe conquered by Cortez and the Spanish. The story features Quetzalcoatl (Plumed Serpent), the god mentioned in Shark Beneath the Reef, *and refers to events and places that existed even before the Aztec Empire. Tula was a legendary city built by the Toltecs who lived in Mexico before being conquered by the Aztecs. Though both the Toltecs and Aztecs were defeated, their myths and memories continue to play an important role in modern-day Mexico.*

UNEQUALED on earth were the serpent-pillared palaces of Tula, one more marvelous than another. There were rooms with walls as gold as the sun, silver as the moon, turquoise and emerald as the sea, pearl-colored as the dawn. Vast halls and chambers were encrusted with seashells or tapestried with birds' feathers. A sparkling bathing palace spanned the river and underground treasure rooms overflowed with jewels, carved jade, and wrought silver and gold.

But the walls of the room where Quetzalcoatl, Plumed Serpent, lived were bare as the walls of a cave. Though he reigned in Tula, and his reign produced abundance, he spent his days in shadow and his nights in utter darkness, fasting, meditating, and performing acts of penance that left him ill for loss of blood. Pages stood outside his door barring entrance to all lest they disturb the king-priest at his devotions.

At the age of nine, Plumed Serpent had avenged the death of his father, the great hunter Cloud Serpent, by slaying his murderers and erecting a temple over his grave. At the age of twenty-seven, he built a house with green crossbeams in Tulancingo, where he did penance for four years. Then the lords and people of Tulsa asked him to rule over them, for there was no one as wise as he. The god Plumed Serpent worshipped was he who dwells in the innermost heaven, known both as She of the Starry Skirt and as He Who Created the World, Lord and Lady of our Flesh. Worshipped was he who dwells in the innermost heaven, where opposites are harmoniously united—to the Lord of the Near and the Far he directed his prayers.

The wisdom and saintliness of their ruler was reflected in the peace and plenty enjoyed by the Toltecs. Although they were said to be taller and longer-limbed than ordinary men, the squash that grew on their vines were so big around that a man could not take one up in his arms and hope to touch the fingers of one hand with the other. Ears of corn were so huge that only one could be carried at a time. Cotton grew in many colors—red, yellow, dark gold, pink, purple, green, blue-green, deep blue, and orange. In flowering cacao trees roosted birds of every species, their plumage bright as polished stones and gay as wild flowers.

Science and the arts also flourished under Plumed Serpent's guidance. The wise Toltecs discovered the long calendar called the Count of the Year and the short calendar called the Count of Days and Destinies. They could predict lucky and unlucky days, knowing how the heavens move and the names of all the stars. Their work with feathers and jewels has never been surpassed. And this pursuit of knowledge and beauty, along with their enjoyment of the fruits of the earth, followed the paths of peace. Plumed Serpent taught his people to love one another and human blood was no longer shed on the altars of sacrifice. But at the same time the jealous nature of a warrior god was roused. Tezcatlipoca, Smoking Mirror, set his heart on ruling Tula in Plumed Serpent's place.

One day a young man dressed in the rich robes of a magician appeared at the door of Plumed Serpent's cell. No one recognized him. Certainly no one suspected he could be a god. He carried something that was wrapped up in many finely embroidered pieces of cloth.

"Tell our lord Plumed Serpent that I would show him his image," said the sorcerer to the pages on guard. His voice was commanding, his eyes as black and threatening as obsidian knives. But the page who went to announce the stranger to his master returned to tell the young magician, "Our lord wishes you to show us his image first."

Smiling, the sorcerer shook his head.

"I can show it to none," he said, "but our lord Plumed Serpent himself."

In this way he excited the penitent's curiosity, and when the page came back a second time the magician was permitted to pass.

With eyes used to the somber light of his quarters, Plumed Serpent studied the stranger's handsome face.

"What is this," he asked, "my image that you carry about with you? A man's image, his face and his heart, is a secret to all but the Lord of Duality. What can you show me?"

"Yourself," replied the magician.

The man of meditation smiled faintly. "Myself," he muttered. "And what am I? I weep. I pray. I feel pain and joy. But these are like dew that the sun dries up on the meadow. When they vanish, I am dry grass, my season passed, my little time used up. If life is a dream, what am I? If I wake again, what will I be? Is that the mysterious image you can show me?"

One by one, the magician removed the cloths that covered the object he held in his hand until he brought to light a mirror, the first Plumed Serpent had ever seen. Staring at its shining surface, Plumed Serpent drew back in horror. Many years had passed that he had not taken account of before. Forgotten was his inner self, so great was his surprise at seeing his body's reflection.

"That," he asked the magician, "is how others see me?"

The young man nodded.

The old man covered his eyes.

"I am ugly," he moaned. "My beard is like twisted fibers. My face is like rotting wood. My body is as crooked and spotty as a lizard's. What happened to my youth?" Then dashing the mirror to the floor, he cried out, "Leave my sight! Let no one look at me from this day hence!"

The magician left Plumed Serpent's cell satisfied that he had found the penitent proud and easy to injure. Plumed Serpent himself began a life of even greater seclusion than before. He had a mask made to cover his face, and no one could approach him unless he was wearing his mask.

Meanwhile, Smoking Mirror wandered at will about the city, creating havoc and causing death. Disguised as a young merchant from the Huastec Mountains, he caught the eye of the daughter of a mighty lord and so conquered her heart that she grew sick with longing for him. In the end, her father could do nothing but let her marry the hated barbarian, though their marriage caused much grumbling and ill feelings among friends, peers, and relatives. Another time Smoking Mirror sat down in the marketplace with a puppet dressed in a loincloth, cape, and collar of precious stones, and caused the puppet to dance with such lifelike grace the Toltecs trampled one another to death in their eagerness to see it. Another, Smoking Mirror arrayed himself in golden plumage and played upon a drum, calling all to dance behind him. When many had gathered, he led them outside the city, up to the cliffs, and the people in their frenzy danced over the edge, turning to stones in the ravine.

In his palace, Plumed Serpent grew weaker daily. Ill and depressed, he no longer practiced his devotions with the purity of heart he had once known. A heavy feeling of loss and failure haunted him. Where had life gone? he asked himself. Is death an escape or an ending? Does the heart of man simply vanish like the ever-withering flowers?

One day a page entered his room to say that an old man had come to see the priest-king.

"Let him come in," Plumed Serpent murmured at once. "I've been alone for many days and am becoming weary of life."

So Smoking Mirror, disguised as an ancient, was once more able to approach him.

"How are you, my son and lord?" he asked upon entering.

Plumed Serpent groaned.

"You suffer unnecessarily," the old man went on, seating himself beside the penitent. "Your body can grow young again in a flash. Your spirit can soar free. Old age and pain are illusions, as you will see upon taking the medicine I have brought you. Drink this—"

He offered Plumed Serpent a cup that he had brought hidden in his robes, but Plumed Serpent pushed it aside, saying, "I am fasting today."

"It is healthful and invigorating," the old man went on persuasively. "Recover your strength. Then you will be able to return to your saintly devotions with renewed force. A drop at least won't harm you. You'll see at once how this medicine was sent by the gods for just such as you. Dip your finger into the cup. Just taste."

His will weakened, Plumed Serpent did as the stranger urged him. Sucking his finger, he found that the liquid in the cup had a good taste and gave him the pleasant tingling of returning health. He smiled a little and said, "I will drink one cup."

But one cup was just enough to go to his head, and having finished it, he consented to another. Then he asked for a third and a fourth, shouting uproariously for the fifth. Feeling himself young and strong again, he sang and invited others to come and share his joy. "Go," he cried out to them, "and tell my sister to join us. Tell her to bring meat and fruit, for we are very merry here and even the gods do not scorn a feast!"

Obediently, Plumed Serpent's sister joined him. She, too, led a pious life, devoting her days and nights to honoring the gods in their temples. But after she had drunk Smoking Mirror's wine, she became forgetful of her duties and day passed into night without the proper ceremonies being observed. Brother and sister forgot to take the ritual bath. The sun disappeared without their knowledge, let alone their prayers. The firewood lay heaped about the altar but neither priest nor priestess set it ablaze. When dawn came, they neglected the sacrifice of quails.

Only when they had slept and awakened did they realize what foolish and sinful things they had done while their heads were muddled with wine. Plumed Serpent wept, and the bitter echo of a song he had sung the night before returned to his confused and tortured thoughts—

My house of precious plumes,
My house of yellow feathers,
My house of coral,
I must leave you.
Sorrow, sorrow!

The song ran through his thoughts all day until at last he called together his servants and his dwarfs and gave them orders to bring wood and heap it up in his palaces, for he meant to burn them to the ground. The cacao trees that grew in his gardens he turned into thorny cactus plants. His birds with breasts of flame and tail feathers like jade he set free. In many colored clouds they rose above the clouds of smoke, and following in their wake, Plumed Serpent turned his footsteps toward the rainlands and the country of boats. Outside the city, he paused a moment under a tall, thick-trunked tree and asked his page for a mirror.

"Yes," he nodded, no longer afraid of what he saw reflected there, "I am old."

Then he departed toward the east, leaving Tula to Smoking Mirror. And when he reached the sea after a long time of wandering, he set out on the waters alone, on a raft of serpents, bound for the red and black Land of Wisdom. But others say that when he came to the coast he set himself afire and that all the birds of the sky flocked to see his sacrifice. When the flames died down, Plumed Serpent's heart rose out of the ashes and soared up to heaven, where it became the sun's companion, the morning star.

from

Call It Courage

Armstrong Sperry

The ancient Polynesians depended upon their skill with the canoe to navigate the Pacific Islands, and to gather fish from the ocean. But Mafatu was afraid of the ocean. His mother had been killed by an ocean storm, and since that day Mafatu had avoided the water. Yet the ocean is life to the island tribes, and there is no place for a boy who will not go out and fish or participate in raids on other islands. Determined to conquer his fear, Mafatu sets off in a canoe with only his dog, Uri, to keep him company. Unfortunately, an ocean storm, like the one that killed his mother, comes up about him. His canoe destroyed, Mafatu is stranded on a deserted island.

THE days passed in a multitude of tasks that kept Mafatu busy from dawn till dark. His lean-to grew into a three-sided house with bamboo walls and a thatch of palm leaves. The fourth wall was open to the breezes of the lagoon. It was a trim little house and he was proud of it. A roll of woven mats lay on the floor; there was a shelf in the wall with three bowls cut from coconut shells; bone fishhooks dangled from a peg; there was a coil of tough sennit, many feet long; an extra *pareu* of tapa waterproofed with gum of the *artu* tree, for wet weather. All day long the wind played through the openings in the bamboo walls and at night lizards scurried through the thatch with soft rustlings.

One morning, wandering far down the beach, Mafatu came upon a sheltered cove. His heart gave a leap of joy; for there, white-gleaming in the sun, was all that remained of the skeleton of a whale. It might not have meant very much to you or to me; but to Mafatu it meant knives and fishhooks galore, splintered bone for darts and spears, a shoulder blade for an ax. It was a veritable treasure trove. The boy leaped up and down in his excitement. "Uri!" he shouted. "We're rich! Come—help me drag these bones home!"

His hands seemed all thumbs in his eagerness; he tied as many bones as he could manage into two bundles. One bundle he shouldered himself. The other Uri dragged behind him. And thus they returned to the camp site, weary, but filled with elation. Even the dog seemed to have some understanding of what this discovery meant; or if not, he was at least infected with his master's high spirits. He leaped about like a sportive puppy, yapping until he was hoarse.

Hunger alone drove Mafatu out to the reef to set his trap. He knew that if he was to maintain strength to accomplish all that lay ahead he must have fish to add to his diet of fruit. But often as he set his trap far out by the barrier-reef, the hammerhead would approach, roll over slightly in passing, and the cold gleam of its eye filled Mafatu with dread and anger.

"Wait, you!" the boy threatened darkly, shaking his fist at the *ma'o*. "Wait until I have my knife! You will not be so brave then, Ma'o. You will run away when you see it flash."

But the morning that the knife was finished, Mafatu did not feel so brave as he would have liked. He hoped he would never see the hammerhead again. Paddling out to the distant reef, he glanced down from time to time at the long-bladed knife where it hung about his neck by a cord of sennit. It wasn't, after all, such a formidable weapon. It was only a knife made by a boy from a whale's rib.

Uri sat on the edge of the raft, sniffing at the wind. Mafatu always took his dog along, for Uri howled unmercifully if he were left behind. And Mafatu had come to rely upon the companionship of the little yellow dog. The boy talked with the animal as if he were another person, consulting with him, arguing, playing when there was time for play. They were very close, these two.

This morning as they approached the spot where the fish trap was anchored, Mafatu saw the polished dorsal of the hated hammerhead circling slowly in the water. It was like a triangle of black basalt, making a little furrow in the water as it passed.

"*Aiá*, Ma'o!" the boy shouted roughly, trying to bolster up his courage. "I have my knife today, see! Coward who robs traps—catch your own fish!"

The hammerhead approached the raft in leisurely fashion; it rolled over slightly, and its gaping jaws seemed to curve in a yawning grin. Uri ran to the edge of the raft, barking furiously; the hair on the dog's neck stood up in a bristling ridge. The shark, unconcerned, moved away. Then with a whip of its powerful tail it rushed at the bamboo fish trap and seized it in its jaws. Mafatu was struck dumb. The hammerhead shook the trap as a terrier might shake a rat. The boy watched, fascinated, unable to make a move. He saw the muscles work in the fish's neck as the great tail thrashed the water to fury. The trap splintered into bits, while the fish within escaped only to vanish into the shark's mouth. Mafatu was filled with impotent rage. The hours he had spent making that trap— But all he could do was shout threats at his enemy.

Uri was running from one side of the raft to the other, furious with excitement. A large wave sheeted across the reef. At that second the dog's shift in weight tipped the raft at a perilous angle. With a helpless yelp, Uri slid off into the water. Mafatu sprang to catch him but he was too late.

Instantly the hammerhead whipped about. The wave slewed the raft away. Uri, swimming frantically, tried to regain it. There was desperation in the brown eyes—the puzzled eyes so faithful and true. Mafatu strained forward. His dog. His companion. . . . The hammerhead was moving in slowly. A mighty rage stormed through the boy. He gripped his knife. Then he was over the side in a clean-curving dive.

Mafatu came up under his enemy. The shark spun about. Its rough hide scraped the flesh from the boy's shoulder. In that instant Mafatu stabbed. Deep, deep into the white belly. There was a terrific impact. Water lashed to foam. Stunned, gasping, the boy fought for life and air.

It seemed that he would never reach the surface. *Aué*, his lungs would burst! . . . At last his head broke water. Putting his face to the surface, he saw the great shark turn over, fathoms deep. Blood flowed from the wound in its belly. Instantly gray shapes rushed in—other sharks, tearing the wounded hammerhead to pieces.

Uri—where was he? Mafatu saw his dog then. Uri was trying to pull himself up on the raft. Mafatu seized him by the scruff and dragged him up to safety. Then he caught his dog to him and hugged him close, talking to him foolishly. Uri yelped for joy and licked his master's cheek.

It wasn't until Mafatu reached shore that he realized what he had done. He had killed the *ma'o* with his own hand, with naught but a bone knife. He could never have done it for himself. Fear would have robbed his arm of all strength. He had done it for Uri, his dog. And he felt suddenly humble, with gratitude.

from

White Shark

Peter Benchley

Simon Chase, a marine biologist, has tagged a pregnant white shark with an electronic tracking device. Together with his old friend, Tall Man, and his son, Max, they follow the shark—hoping to witness the birth of a shark in the wild.

SUDDENLY Tall Man straightened up. "We got trouble, Simon," he said. "A couple of yahoos are yammering over channel sixteen that they've just hooked Jaws."

. . . "Can you tell where they are?"

"About three miles to the northeast, sounds like, just this side of Block."

"Let's go," Chase said. He shoved the lobster pot overboard and tossed the rope and buoy after it.

Tall Man put the boat in gear, pushed the throttle forward and, as the boat leaped ahead, turned it in a tight arc and headed toward Block Island.

Max held on to the railing and bent his knees as the bow of the boat thumped into the waves. "Do you think it's our shark?" he shouted to his father.

"I'd bet on it," Chase said. "She's the only one we've seen."

The boat rose up onto a plane and skimmed over the surface. The hump of Block Island grew swiftly larger, and as they watched, a small white dot took shape on the surface of the sea and soon became the hull of a boat.

"What are you gonna do?" Max asked. "What *can* you do?"

"I'm not sure, Max," Chase said, staring grimly ahead. "But something."

"They're two kids," Tall Man said, looking through a pair of binoculars. "Sixteen, eighteen, maybe . . . fishin' from a twenty-foot outboard. Stupid . . . They better *hope* they don't land the shark; it'll turn that boat into splinters."

Tall Man throttled back as he approached the outboard, then took the boat out of gear and let it idle thirty or forty yards off the outboard's port side.

One boy sat in a fighting chair in the stern, the butt of his rod snugged into a socket between his legs. The rod was bent nearly to the breaking point, and the line led straight out behind the boat: the shark was near the surface, but still fifty yards or more away. The other boy stood forward, at the console, turning the wheel and using the gears to keep the stern of the outboard facing the shark.

"Can he really catch a shark that big?" Max asked. "On a fishing rod?"

"If he knows what he's doing," Chase said. "He's using a tuna rig, probably sixty- or eighty-pound test line with a steel leader."

"But you said the shark weighed a ton."

"He can still wear her out. Great whites aren't great fighters, they're not true game fish. They just pull and pull and finally give up."

As they watched, the boy with the rod tried to reel in some line, but the weight was too great, and the drum of the reel skidded beneath the spool of line. So the boy at the console put the outboard in reverse, backing down toward the shark, giving the angler slack to reel in.

As Chase had feared, the boys knew what they were doing.

"Get closer," he said to Tall Man. "I want to have a talk with them."

Tall Man maneuvered so that the stern of the boat was within ten yards of the side of the outboard. Chase walked aft and stood at the transom.

"What've you got there?" he asked.

"Jaws, man," the boy at the console said. "Biggest . . . white shark you ever seen."

"What're you gonna do with it?"

"Catch it . . . sell the jaws."

"How're you gonna get it aboard that little boat?"

"Don't have to . . . gonna kill it, then tow it in."

"Kill it how? That's one big angry shark."

"With this." The boy reached under the console and brought out a shotgun. "All we have to do is get close enough to him for one clean shot."

Chase paused, considering, then said, "Did you know he's a she?"

"Huh?"

"That shark is a female, and she's pregnant. We've tagged her, we've been studying her. If you kill her, you're not just killing her, you're killing her and her children and her children's children."

"It's a fish," the boy said. "Why should I . . . "

"Because white sharks are very rare . . . endangered, even. I'll make you a deal. You cut that shark away—"

. . . "I been busting my hump—"

"—and I'll get your names in the paper for helping the Institute. You'll get a lot more mileage than if you just kill her."

"Not a chance." The boy with the rod yelled over his shoulder, "Come back some more, Jimmy. He's takin' line again."

The boy at the console put the outboard in reverse, and Chase saw the angle of the line increase as the boat neared the shark.

"Dad," Max said, "we've gotta *do* something."

"Yeah," Chase said, leaning on the bulwark as he felt rage rise within him. The problem was, there was nothing he *could* do, not legally anyway, for the boys were breaking no law. And yet he knew that if he let this happen, he would never forgive himself. He turned away and went below.

When he returned, he was carrying a mask and a pair of flippers, and a pair of wire cutters was stuck in the belt of his shorts.

" . . . Simon . . ." Tall Man said from the flying bridge.

"Where is she, Tall?"

Tall Man pointed. "About twenty yards thataway, but you don't—"

"She's so worn out and confused, she won't pay any attention to me. Last thing she wants to do is eat anybody."

"You know that, do you?"

"Sure," Chase said, forcing a smile and pulling on his flippers. "At least, I *hope* that."

"Dad!" Max said, as Chase's intent suddenly dawned on him. "You can't—"

"Trust me, Max." Chase pulled the mask over his face and rolled backward off the bulwark.

The driver of the outboard saw the splash as Chase fell into the water, and he shouted, "Hey! What's . . . he up to?"

"What you shoulda done way back when," Tall Man said.

The boy picked up his shotgun and cocked it. "You get him back, or—"

"Put that away . . . " said Tall Man, in a voice as flat and hard as slate, "or I'll come over there and make you eat it."

The boy looked up at the huge dark man towering over him on the flying bridge of the much larger boat, and he lowered the shotgun.

Chase located the line feeding down from the outboard and followed it with his eyes until he saw the shark. He took three or four deep breaths on the surface, held the final one and thrust himself downward with his flippers.

The shark had stopped fighting, for in its initial thrashing it had rolled up into the steel leader and then into the line itself, and now it was circled with monofilament strands that pressed into its flesh. It lolled on its side, perhaps resting for a final, futile attempt to escape, perhaps already resigned to death.

Chase swam to it, staying away from the snarls of line until he was within arm's reach of the tail of the shark.

He had never before swum in the open with a great white shark. He had seen them from the safety of a cage, had touched their tails as they swept by the bars in pursuit of hanging baits, had marveled at their power, but he had never been alone in the sea with this ultimate predator.

He permitted himself a moment to run his hand down the steel-smooth skin of the back, then backward against the grain of the dermal denticles, which felt like rubbing sandpaper. He found his tagging dart and its tiny transmitter, still securely set in the skin behind the dorsal fin. Then he leaned over the shark; its eye gazed at him with neither fear nor hostility, but with a blank and fathomless neutrality.

There were six loops around the shark—one of steel, five of monofilament—starting just forward of the tail, ending just forward of the pectoral fins. Chase hovered above the shark, nearly lying upon its back, took the wire cutters from his belt and cut the loops one by one. As each muscle group in the torpedo-like body sensed freedom, it began to shudder and ripple. When the last loop was gone, the shark swung downward, suspended only by the wire in its mouth that led to the hook deep in its belly. Chase reached his hand into the mouth of the shark and snipped the wire.

The shark was free. It began to fall, upside down, and for a moment Chase feared that it had died, that the lack of forward motion had deprived it of oxygen and it had asphyxiated. But then the tail swept once from side to side, the shark rolled over and its mouth opened as water rushed over its gills. It turned in a circle, its eye fixed on Chase, and rose toward him.

It came slowly, relentlessly, unexcited, unafraid, its mouth half open, its tail thrusting it forward.

Chase did not turn or flee or backpedal. He faced the shark and watched its eyes, knowing that the only warning he would have of an imminent attack would be the rotating of its eyeballs, an instinctive protection against the teeth or claws of its victim.

He heard his temples pounding and felt arrows of adrenaline shooting through his limbs.

The shark came on, face-to-face, until it was four feet from Chase, then suddenly rolled onto its side, presenting its snow-white belly distended with young, and angled downward, like a banking fighter plane, disappearing into the blue-green depths.

Chase watched until the shark was gone. Then he surfaced, snatched a few gasping breaths and made his way back to the boat. He pulled himself out of the water, and as he sat on the swimstep to remove his flippers, he noticed that the pulpit of the Institute boat was hovering over the hull of the outboard. He heard Tall Man say, "So, we got a deal, right? The story is, you hooked the shark, saw that it was tagged and reported it to us. We tell the papers what fine citizens you are."

The sullen boys stood in the stern of the outboard, and one of them said, "Yeah, okay. . . ."

Tall Man looked down, saw that Chase was aboard, then put the boat in reverse. "Thanks," he called to the boys.

Chase passed Max his flippers and climbed up through the door in the transom.

Max looked angry. "That was really dumb, Dad," he said. "You could've—"

"It was a calculated risk, Max," Chase said. "That's what dealing with wild animals is. I was pretty sure she wouldn't bite me; I made a judgment that the risk was worth taking, to save the life of that mama shark."

"But suppose you'd been wrong. Is a shark's life worth as much as yours?"

"That's not the point; the point is, I knew what I had to do. The Bible may say man has dominion over animals, but that doesn't mean we've got the right to wipe them off the face of the earth."

Sharks: The Perfect Hunters

Margret Harris

THERE is no creature in the sea more terrifying than the shark. People have had superstitions and made up myths about sharks that have been passed along for centuries. Stories have been told of sharks large enough to smash holes in the sides of great ships. Sharks have been said to hurl themselves from the water to snatch some poor sailor from his boat.

Magical stories of old Hawaii tell of killer sharks who can change into human form, destroy their enemies, and then return to the sea as sharks. Even today, these ancient creatures of the sea are thought by some to be cruel, ever-hungry hunters of human flesh. These are some of the myths. What is the truth about sharks?

Sharks were among the earliest animals on earth. We know there were sharks swimming the oceans at least 140 million years ago. While no shark bodies this old have been found, fossil teeth of prehistoric sharks have been discovered. Teeth from the *great white shark* have been found that are six inches long. There are people who believe these triangle-shaped teeth are from sharks 80 to 90 feet long. Sharks this size would have huge jaws capable of swallowing a Volkswagen!

As exciting as the idea of a 90-foot shark sounds, it probably isn't true. The largest fish in the world is a shark—the whale shark—that sometimes grows to almost 65 feet in length. The whale shark is not a flesh-eater. It feeds on ocean plants and small fish.

Norwegian adventurer Thor Heyerdahl once met up with the *whale shark*. On his sailing voyage from Peru to Polynesia, Heyerdahl and his crew spotted fish "bigger than elephants." In fact, at one point during his trip, Heyerdahl said one of these giant monsters was visible from both sides of the boat at the same time. The largest known flesh-eating shark measures about 40 feet. Standing on its tail a shark this size would stretch up as tall as a four-story building.

Perhaps the 90-foot monster of man's imagination *did* exist at one time. But there is no proof. That monster shark remains a legend. On the other hand, there *are* fossil teeth that probably came from a race of killer sharks that must have been more than 60 feet long. Killers that size no longer roam the seas.

Sharks are not bony fish. Their bodies are made up of *cartilage*—the kind of firm, rubbery material that forms the tip of your nose. The dead shark's body, therefore, decays quickly and leaves no fossil bones for scientists to study. What we know of the age and life of sharks comes from studies of fossil teeth and living creatures.

The shark has been called "the perfect hunter." A major reason is the shark's jaw and its several rows of teeth. Most rows are slanted toward the rear of the mouth. Each row is slightly larger than the last. When the shark bites, its sharp, sawlike teeth easily slice through tough flesh. The angled rear teeth hold on fast to the victim. It is easy to get something into a shark's mouth but impossible to get it back out. The shark always has its original number of teeth. As a tooth is lost, another grows to replace it. A *tiger shark* is said to grow 24,000 individual teeth over a ten-year period of time.

In addition to the jaw, the shark's entire body makes it "the perfect hunter." Its sleek, smooth form is as streamlined as a torpedo for speedy movement through the water. Sharks swim more than 30 knots an hour (equal to land speeds of almost 35 mph). In the words of Jacques Cousteau, famous underwater explorer: "[the shark body] is fluid, weaving from side to side . . . his head moves slowly from left to right, right to left, timed to the rhythm of his motion through the water. Only the [shark's] eye is fixed . . . on me in order not to lose sight, for a fraction of a second, of his enemy."

Not all sharks are killers. There are some, like the giant whale sharks, that actually refuse to attack people. Stories are told of sailors taunting these sharks—daring them to attack. Even this did not make the whale sharks angry. In fact, whale sharks will go out of their way to avoid bumping into small boats or divers.

Eugenie Clark and the Sleeping Sharks

Margery Facklam

SUNLIGHT sparkled on bright blue-green water as a small boat dropped anchor. Three divers wearing black wet suits adjusted their scuba gear. One diver leaned over the side of the boat and peered into the water. It was so clear he could see the rainbow assortment of fishes swimming around the coral reef.

"Sharks below," he called.

"No problem," a second diver answered calmly. "Use this," she said, handing cans of shark repellent to the others.

When they had sprayed themselves all over with the repellent, the divers put on their masks and flipped backward out of the boat into the warm water. Two tiger sharks began to circle the divers. Silently they picked up speed to attack, but as they closed in on the swimmers, they slammed on invisible brakes. Suddenly their mouths seemed to be frozen open. They shook their heads as though trying to get rid of something. And the divers went about exploring the coral reef, unconcerned about the sharks.

So far, that scene is only make-believe. There is no shark repellent that really keeps sharks away, but there may be soon because Dr. Eugenie Clark was curious about a little fish called the Moses sole.

In 1960, Eugenie was netting fish in the Red Sea when she came across the fish known scientifically as *Pardachirus;* local fishermen called it the Moses sole. When she touched the fish, a milky substance oozed from the pores along its fins. It was slippery, and her fingers felt tingly and tight, the way they might feel if they fell asleep.

The Moses sole is a flatfish, like the flounder you buy at the market, and it got its name from a traditional story told in Israel. According to the legend, when Moses parted the Red Sea, this little fish was caught in the middle and split in half. Each half became a sole.

Eugenie is an ichthyologist, a scientist who studies fish. She was working at the Marine Laboratory at the Hebrew University in Elat, Israel, when she decided to find out more about the sole's poison. A scientist had reported the poisonous substance in 1871, but no one had studied it further. When Eugenie tested it on sea urchins, starfish, and reef fishes, she found that small doses killed these creatures quickly. She began to wonder how it would work on larger fishes, especially sharks.

Three reef whitetip sharks lived in a tank at the laboratory, and they ate anything dropped into the water. One day as Eugenie was experimenting with the fish, she found one small Moses sole that had not been completely "milked" of its poison. She put a string through its gills, which did not hurt it, and lowered the fish into the shark's tank. The moment the sole touched the water, the sharks swept toward it with mouths open wide. But when they got within a few feet of the fish on the string, the sharks' jaws seemed to be frozen open. They dashed away, shaking their heads as though trying to get rid of something awful. For six hours Eugenie watched the sharks approach the sole, and the reactions were the same each time the sharks swam near the poisonous fish.

The use of this poison as a shark repellent was an exciting idea. So far everything invented to keep sharks away has not worked on all sharks all the time. Streams of air bubbles used as a barrier along beaches eventually attracted sharks, who seemed to enjoy the feeling of the bubbles as they swam through them. Different dyes that swimmers can release in the water only hide the swimmer from the shark temporarily but cannot keep a really hungry shark away. Lifeboats on ships and Navy planes are sometimes equipped with plastic bags large enough to hold a person. Stranded in the water, the person inflates the top ring and crawls into the tubelike bag. A shark cannot follow the scent of a human inside this bag, nor can it see kicking legs or blood from a wound. But such bags are not carried as regular equipment by swimmers at an ocean beach. A substance that can be sprayed on, the way mosquito repellent is, would be perfect.

But before Eugenie could experiment further on the Moses sole, she had to leave the Elat laboratory, and other work claimed her attention for many years. It wasn't until 1974 that she was able to collect some of the fish and test the shark-stopping poison. After dozens of experiments in tanks and in the sea, a final test was arranged to find out how free-swimming sharks reacted to the live Moses sole.

An eighty-foot shark line, with ten shorter lines dropping from it, was stretched close to the rocky Israeli coastline three feet underwater at a point where a ledge dropped off to a depth of one thousand feet. Each of the ten dropper lines was baited with parrot fish, groupers, nonpoisonous flatfish, and the Moses sole. As Eugenie, her fourteen-year-old son, and other assistants snorkeled quietly along the underwater ledge and watched the sharks approach the bait at dawn or sunset, they saw the poison at work.

One by one the fish were gulped down by hungry sharks, but the Moses sole remained untouched. When Eugenie wiped the skin of a Moses sole with alcohol to remove the poison and tossed the fish into the water, a shark would instantly eat it. It was an exciting discovery—a substance that could really stop a shark. Further work is being done now to make a chemical compound like the poison of the Moses sole that can be used as a reliable commercial shark repellent.

Eugenie knew she wanted to be an ichthyologist long before she knew the word meant "someone who studies fish." Her father died when she was very small, and she lived in New York City with her mother. When her mother had to work on Saturdays, Eugenie went to the old aquarium in Battery Park at the tip of Manhattan. The hours went quickly for her as she watched the colorful reef fishes and the graceful sea turtles. It wasn't long before she had her own collection of guppies and swordtail platys, and she became the youngest member of the Queens County Aquarium Society. She learned to keep careful records of her fish and their scientific names.

All during elementary school and high school, her mother encouraged her in her new interest. When she went to Hunter College in New York for a degree in biology, Mrs. Clark, aware of the limited job possibilities for women, suggested that Eugenie add typing and shorthand to her studies. But Eugenie never had the time or interest to do it. When she graduated from Hunter College during World War II, there were not many jobs for biologists, so she worked for a while at the Celanese Corporation as a chemist and attended graduate school at night.

She wrote later on, "In the field of science, a Ph.D. degree is handy to have although not absolutely necessary. One of the most brilliant and accomplished ichthyologists in the country never went to college, although later he became a university professor. But a person without a formal education has a more difficult time proving his worth, especially when applying for a position. A Ph.D. among your qualifications helps start things out on the right foot. I hoped to get this degree . . . my career had enough other disadvantages for a woman."

In 1947, the U.S. Fish and Wildlife Service was planning a survey of the Philippine Island area for possible fisheries. They needed a person who knew fish and chemistry. Eugenie was qualified. She applied for the job and got it.

"Several people were surprised that a girl had been hired for the job. Then it was called to someone's attention in Washington that I was the only female scientist on the program. Some commotion followed. I got as far as Hawaii, but my passport was mysteriously delayed because, they told me, the FBI had to check my Oriental [Eugenie's mother is Japanese] origin and connections. As far as I know they are still checking. They never did tell me I was cleared. After weeks of waiting, I accepted my fate and handed in my resignation to waiting hands. They hired a man in my place."

Being stranded in Hawaii was no hardship for Eugenie. For an ichthyologist, the freedom to dive among the fascinating fishes around the Hawaiian volcanic reefs was as satisfying as being a cat free to roll in a meadow of catnip. But even that ended. She said later, "The longer you put off graduate studies, the harder it is to find the time and enthusiasm to go back to school." So she went back.

It takes years of study and research to complete a Ph.D. Very often the original research requires going into the field to learn about the subject first-hand.

"Women scientists have to buck some difficulties when it comes to field work," said Eugenie, "but I had one decided advantage. A man in my position often has a family to support and is not free to travel. I was independent and free to go anywhere and do anything I liked, and there was only my own neck to risk."

Eugenie went many places. She learned to dive while studying at Scripps Institute of Oceanography in California. She used her diving skills constantly in Micronesia in the Pacific Ocean, where she collected the *plectognaths* she was studying. These are small fish that live mostly in tropical waters near coral reefs. They include the triggerfish, porcupine fish, puffer, filefish, and boxfish.

One of her research fellowships took her to the Red Sea, where she found the Moses sole and collected the elusive garden eels that burrow in the ocean bottom. They are long, smooth fish that sway gently with the water currents as they feed upon small ocean creatures.

In Cairo, Egypt, Eugenie married a doctor she had met during her studies in the United States. When they returned to the states, Eugenie began the less glamorous part of being a scientist—sorting through notes and writing the scientific results of things she had found. And she began to raise a family.

In 1955, she was delighted to be asked to start a marine laboratory in Florida. Her husband was ready to open a medical office, and he agreed that Florida would be a good place to live. With their first two children, they moved to Florida's west coast, and Eugenie became the director of the Cape Haze Marine Laboratory. At first the laboratory was only a small wooden building, twelve by twenty feet, built on skids so it could be moved if the first site did not work out. There was a dock and a boat for collecting. Eugenie decided her first job should be to collect and identify all the local fishes.

The day after she arrived, she received a phone call from a doctor who needed shark livers for cancer research. She checked with the man who was going to handle the boat, and even before supplies were unpacked, they were in the shark-hunting business.

There are about 250 different sharks in the world, ranging in size from the 24-inch dogfish studied in biology classes to the 60-foot giant whale shark that eats plankton and is so gentle that divers have hung onto its fins for a short ride. In between are the man-eaters we hear horror stories about. All the sharks belong to a group of fishes called cartilaginous. They have skeletons made not of bone but of cartilage, that bendable tissue our ears and noses are made of. And all the sharks are torpedo-shaped predators. They have many sets of razor-sharp teeth that they can fold back into a nonbiting position or thrust forward, ready to slice easily into prey. When a tooth is lost, another moves into place quite quickly.

The shark's always-staring eyes give it an evil appearance. It cannot blink or close its eyes for sleep, but it has a membrane that can cover the eye for protection.

Eugenie and her assistant began collecting some of the eighteen species of sharks found off the west coast of Florida. As she dissected hammerhead, nurse, lemon, and sand sharks on the dock, her children, neighbors, and children of visiting scientists watched. Sometimes she gave them jobs to do—measuring parts of the intestines, washing out a shark stomach, or hosing the dock after the dissection. Some of the sharks brought in on lines survived, and Eugenie wanted to know as much about the live animals as she knew about the organs she was weighing and measuring.

A stockaded pen, forty by seventy feet, was built next to the dock to hold the live sharks. A tiger shark, named Hazel, and a reddish color nurse shark, named Rosy, were two of the first guests in the pen, and a new problem arose. Nosy visitors, ignoring signs and fences, poked around and teased the animals. Eugenie was worried that both people and sharks would be hurt. When several of the sharks were killed by trespassers, Eugenie began to talk to groups in the community, especially at schools. She explained what sharks eat and how they live. Whenever people know about an animal, they fear it less. Soon the newspapers labeled her the "shark lady." It is a name that has stayed with her in spite of all her research with other sea creatures.

It wasn't long before Eugenie was involved in finding out how sharks learn. She enjoyed working with the live sharks day after day and getting to know the individual personalities of the animals.

When she set up experiments in which sharks would have to hit a target to receive the reward of food, one scientist warned her, "Don't be discouraged. It may take months." But he was wrong. The sharks learned quickly. When two lemon sharks learned that they could press an empty target and get food for it, Eugenie thought up harder problems for them to solve.

She trained them to swim to the end of the seventy-foot pen to pick up food after they pressed the target; and the female shark, who usually hung back and waited for the male to go first, quickly learned that if she circled the food drop area, she could pick up the male's reward while he was still at the target.

Eugenie stopped the tests during the winter months when the sharks lost interest in food, but she found that the sharks remembered everything they had learned when spring training began. She moved on to more complicated learning. She used targets of different sizes, shapes, and designs, and she found that sharks of the same species, like other animals, have great individual differences. Some are smarter than others.

Scientists from all over the world visited the Cape Haze laboratory, studying everything from parasites on sharks to microscopic life on algae. By the time Eugenie had been the laboratory's director for ten years, she had four children who enjoyed diving and helping her underwater explorations.

When Eugenie heard that there were "sleeping" sharks a diver could swim right up to, she was determined to find out more about them. With her daughter, Aya, and some research assistants, she went to Mexico's beautiful Isla Mujeres off the tip of the Yucatán Peninsula. There, in the warm, clear underwater caves, she found the great, sleek sharks of the requiem family—the notorious man-eaters. They were lying on the floor of the caves, looking half-asleep even though their open, staring eyes watched the divers swim toward them.

Ordinarily, these sharks must keep moving. They swim constantly in order to keep the oxygen-rich water flowing through their mouths and out over the gills. When they rest on the bottom, they must pump water over the gills, and that takes more energy than leisurely swimming. But in the caves the sharks were motionless. Even with divers churning up water and sand, and even with the glare of photographers' lights, the sharks acted as though they were tranquilized.

Eugenie and her team measured the depth and temperature of the water in the cave. They mapped the water currents by dropping dyes in the water and following their paths. They took water and rock samples for chemical analysis. And they noticed how clean the sharks looked compared to those caught by local fishermen. These cave sharks were not infested with the parasites found on most sharks.

They watched the "shark's faithful housekeeper," the small remora fish, as it worked around the eyes and mouths and into the gill slits of the resting sharks. The remora is a fish whose dorsal fin has evolved into a kind of suction disk on the top of its head. It can hitch a ride on a shark, sea turtle, whale, or even a ship by means of this suction disk. The remora picks up pieces of food dropped by its host. In the caves, however, these remoras worked diligently. Could it be that these "sleeping" sharks gathered in the caves for a health treatment? Were the caves cleaning stations?

Eugenie discovered fresh water seeping into the caves, diluting the sea water. There was less salt in the caves than in the open ocean. She remembered that when she was a kid she would put her saltwater fish into fresh water for a little while so that the parasites would drop off. Perhaps the same thing was happening with the sharks. Maybe these eighteen-foot tiger and reef sharks were intelligent enough to seek comfort in the caves.

Eugenie had taught sharks to ring a bell and push targets for meals and to distinguish right from wrong targets at the Florida laboratory. "Surely," she said, "they are capable of learning that in water of below-normal salinity, a condition they apparently must sense, annoying parasites loosen their grip."

The sharks may not know the water is less salty, but they know it feels good, so they go there. There are three such caves known around Mexico. Recently, some underwater caves full of sharks were reported around Japan. So many divers swarmed into the caves, catching sharks by the hundreds for food, that by the time Eugenie got to Japan to see them, the sharks had learned it was not safe to go to that cleaning station. Another cave was discovered near Japan, but Eugenie and other scientists are keeping its location secret to protect the sharks.

When asked about her life as a scientist, Eugenie said, “Being a scientist and a woman has some advantages, some disadvantages. It balances out. It takes some time to prove yourself initially, but then you get more credit than a man when you do accomplish something. For example, I am a diver, and when I dive into a cave with sharks it seems to be much more amazing than when a man does it.”

The “shark lady” publicity has followed Eugenie, and no matter what she does, people think of her as the spear-carrying shark hunter. But she said, “I get just as excited about the garden eels in the Red Sea. Perhaps the discovery that thrilled me the most was the first hermaphroditic vertebrate, a fish that changes sex.”

Looking for an excuse to go swimming one hot July day, Eugenie decided to take a census of the fish around a certain coral reef near the Cape Haze laboratory. She watched a tiny grouper fish, called *Serranus*. There were dozens of females swollen with eggs that would have to be laid and fertilized. But she could not find any males. No matter how long she followed some of these fish or what time of day she watched, no males appeared.

For a year she found no answers. But after many dives and long hours in the lab looking at fish under the microscope and watching live fish in lab tanks, she finally solved the mystery. *Serranus* is an hermaphrodite—an animal with both male and female parts. There are a few vertebrates that start life as one sex and turn into another, functioning as both in a lifetime, but never at the same time. *Serranus* turned out to be the first vertebrate found in which every individual could function at the same time as a male and female, able to fertilize itself. It seems, however, that this self-fertilization is used only in an emergency when a mate is not available. It was an exciting discovery that will probably lead to other investigations.

Eugenie Clark obviously loves what she does. “If from my research mankind gains some practical application or benefit, this is added delight and satisfaction to my work,” she said. “But this is not what drives me to study late into the night or to watch a fish on the bottom making some strange maneuver until all the air in my scuba tank is gone and I hold my breath for those last few seconds.”

The Poor Boy Was Wrong

John Ciardi

There was a young fellow named Sid
Who thought he knew more than he did.
    He thought that a shark
    Would turn tail if you bark.
So he swam out to try it—poor kid!

The Silver Fish

Shel Silverstein

While fishing in the blue lagoon,
I caught a lovely silver fish,
And he spoke to me, "My boy," quoth he,
"Please set me free and I'll grant your wish;
A kingdom of wisdom? A palace of gold?
Or all the fancies your mind can hold?"
And I said, "O.K.," and I set him free,
But he laughed at me as he swam away,
And left me whispering my wish
Into a silent sea.

Today I caught that fish again
(That lovely silver prince of fishes),
And once again he offered me,
If I would only set him free,
Any one of a number of wishes,
If I would throw him back to the fishes.

He was delicious!

Break, Break, Break

Alfred, Lord Tennyson

Break, break, break,
  On thy cold gray stones, O Sea!
And I would that my tongue could utter
  The thoughts that arise in me.

O, well for the fisherman's boy,
  That he shouts with his sister at play!
O, well for the sailor lad,
  That he sings in his boat on the bay!

And the stately ships go on
  To their haven under the hill;
But O for the touch of a vanish'd hand,
  And the sound of a voice that is still!

Break, break, break,
  At the foot of thy crags, O Sea!
But the tender grace of a day that is dead
  Will never come back to me.

Sea Songs

Myra Cohn Livingston

Crashing on dark shores, drowning, pounding
breaker swallows breaker. Tide follows
tide. Lost in her midnight witchery
moon watches, cresting tall waves, pushing
through mist and blackness the cold waters.

Moon, you have worked long.
Now rest . . .

Mermaids curl in coral beds. Kraken
wind long tentacles, weave tales of lost
sailors sleeping in beams of sunken
ships; tales of bright treasure buried in
silt and the glittering of doubloons.

Moon, you have gone mad.
Be still . . .

Caravels, lashed by tails of mermen
carry old dreams. Galleons, shouldered on
scaly arms, bound over the breakers.
Clouds gather in white mist. All is still.
Pale stars disappear in darkling sky.

Moon, you speak in
strange riddles . . .

Wind rises. Drizzle turns to raindrop.
Sea and sky split with thunder, gale howls.
Heaving ships, plunged into black waters,
vomit saltspray back to hissing seas,
sailing over, up and ever on.

Moon, you cry out with
nightmare . . .

This, Columbus saw beneath ocean
stretching from dark shores to wide, bright sands,
tossed and buffeted by strong iron
chains rusted with blood-red; yet never
waking from dream, he sailed in madness.

Moon, your tale is told
Now sleep . . .

Drowned in foam, faded in the gray mist,
phantoms disappear. A sandpiper
prints the clean morning sand. Pelicans
plunge dive the whitecaps. Across distant
sea swells, sun gurgles, rising in light.

Moon, your shadow
still watches . . .

Fishermen unwind tangled nets, cast
trawls into marbled waters, snaring
schools of fish in their tarred, wet purses,
chumming and charming with live wriggling
anchovy and herring, a day's catch.

Sun, you watch behind
thin clouds.

Tilted umbrellas nod in soft sand.
Patchworks of bright towels sprawl beach picnics.
Surfboards ride the foaming surf. Painted
pails pour water into moated castles,
buried in the lost digs of summer.

Sun, you climb higher
and higher.

Ketches and sloops color the blue days.
Spinnakers of red rig for racing.
Dinghies and catamarans bobbing,
jumbles of masts and booms in dizzy
patterns, billow with walloping sails.

Sun, you smile on
your play.

Wind blows the water into furrows.
Waves leap toward the shore, the crests foaming
white, the whitecaps spraying, splaying,
dashing against pitted rocks, dying
slowly in the thirsty, sponging sands.

Sun, you sink as
you watch.

Under the sand, below the water
sun in spring feeds the floating plankton,
forking light on the drifting seaweeds,
multiplying herring, menhaden,
churning over the salts of the sea.

Sun, you bring life,
you bring food.

Cries of porpoise and dolphin echo
through dark submarine canyons and shelves.
Shrimp crackle, small croakers and drums hiss.
Huge rubber men pry from barnacles
giant scallops and swim with gray sharks.

Here, sun, you can
still see.

Deeper than this, dwell darkness and cold.
Sun cannot probe these underground dungeons
locked by sea devils and dragonfish,
flashing with light, turning on eerie
torches, kaleidoscopes of color.

No sun, no moon
sees here.

Who cries of what lies beyond, beneath
bottom realms? Volcanoes rising from
ocean floor, golden with shells, gray wash
showered from earth, red clay, and wind dust?
Who speaks of mysterious red tides?

Moon, you return
once more . . .

Ghosts raise galley ships on crimson tides.
Sun flees. Foghorn cries to lighthouse.
Wind blows wild storms and over dark waves
mermaids sing bewitching sea songs to
sailors steering wildly toward the moon.

Moon, speak once more
the dreams . . .

The Three Fishers

Charles Kingsley

Three fishers went sailing out into the west—
Out into the west as the sun went down;
Each thought of the woman who loved him the best,
And the children stood watching them out of the town;
For men must work, and women must weep;
And there's little to earn, and many to keep,
Though the harbor bar be moaning.

Three wives sat up in the lighthouse tower,
And trimmed the lamps as the sun went down;
And they looked at the squall, and they looked at the shower,
And the rack it came rolling up, ragged and brown;
But men must work, and women must weep,
Though storms be sudden, and waters deep,
And the harbor bar be moaning.

Three corpses lay out on the shining sands
In the morning gleam as the tide went down,
And the women are watching and wringing their hands,
For those who will never come back to the town;
For men must work, and women must weep—
And the sooner it's over, the sooner to sleep—
And good-by to the bar and its moaning.

from

Between the Devil and the Sea

Brenda A. Johnston

THERE was excitement along the harbor, and James joined the crowds watching the *Royal Lewis*, Philadelphia's own privateer, bringing its captured British vessel into port. Since Philadelphia was the capital of the new nation, James witnessed many auctions of captured British cargo at the wharves and marveled at the proceeds that the captain and the crew shared as a reward. The privateers were not part of the navy, but American pirate ships whose mission was to stop the British merchant ships. Their reward was patriotic glory, the wealthy cargo from the captured ships, and a small monthly allotment as well.

James wanted to join the privateer crew more than anything else in the world, but he had already learned that it was useless to plead with his mother. As he walked home from the docks, he passed the London Coffee House, where he met his friends Larry and Fred standing outside.

"Guess what?" They greeted him in excitement.

"What?" asked James coolly, careful not to betray his curiosity.

"Guess who got signed up for the *Royal Lewis*'s next trip?"

James was interested. "Not you, I know," he said, hoping with all his heart that they were not going before he could.

"Daniel Brewton," they answered him. Daniel was one of their white friends.

"I'm going to sign up, too," said James decisively.

"You're too young," said Fred.

"Daniel and I are the same age almost," said James.

"Your mother'll kill you," declared Larry. "Besides, we already tried."

James left them standing there while he approached a man sitting at a table taking down names. He stood before the man and cleared his throat.

The man looked at him inquiringly for a moment, then asked sharply, "How old are you?"

"Sixteen," said James, thinking fast. He was already nearly six feet tall and walked with a slow, self-confident gait. Black bushy eyebrows framed a lean creamed-coffee face and gave him the appearance of a scowl until one of his slow smiles broke through, lit his eyes, and showed two rows of perfect white teeth. His smiles were rare though, and most of the time his face was expressionless. He had acquired the habit of gazing unfalteringly into a person's eyes while talking, but taking care that none of his own feelings were ever reflected in his dark eyes. He now fixed his gaze on the man and waited.

The man finally shrugged his shoulders and said, "Oh, well. You're on. What's your name?"

"James Forten," he answered quickly, already wondering what he was going to tell his mother.

The man's voice broke through his thoughts. "We sail in three days, James. See you then."

He walked back to his friends and with disdain in every word said, "Well, boys, the *Royal Lewis* and I sail in three days."

They were astonished. "How?" they asked. "What did you say?"

James laughed at their dismay and patted their heads.

"I think," he said, "that you two are just a little too short." He started for home.

In spite of his apprehension about telling his mother the bad news, James was humming with joy when he reached home. His spirits were so high that even Abigail and his mother caught his mood. James put off telling his mother until he had read to her from the Bible that evening. But as he closed the book, he looked at her and started.

"Mother, can I join the crew of the *Royal Lewis?*"

She didn't answer but just returned his direct look. For a panicky moment, he wondered if someone had already told her what he had done. She acted as if she knew.

"They are taking twenty black sailors with them, Mother," he finally said.

She still would not answer. James wildly thought that either she was a mind reader or she had talked to Larry's mother.

"I'm one of the twenty," he said at last, shamefacedly.

His mother folded her arms and shook her head but did not say anything. It was the only time James had ever defied her. Now he felt sorry.

"Is it all right?" he asked, his voice pleading.

"You did what you wanted to do already, didn't you?" She sounded tired.

"Oh, I'll never get a job in the sail loft so long as the war lasts," said James. "Business keeps getting slower and slower. This way I'll get a chance to do lots of things. Travel. Defend my country." His eyes sparkled in excitement, and he suddenly laughed aloud.

"Oh, Mother," he exclaimed, "I've always wanted to ride in a ship and see the sails from the other side."

"But, James," she said, her voice almost breaking, "it's so dangerous."

"Not for our ship," said James, "the *Royal Lewis*, commanded by Captain Decatur—King of the Sea."

"Promise me," his mother said, finally relenting, "that you will read your Bible every night. You'll never know how much your father wanted you to be able to read."

"I promise," said James. "Only, Mother, no one can forget how to read. It's like forgetting how to walk."

Three days later James went down to the docks, taking only the clothes he wore on his back, his mother's Bible, and a bag of marbles. On the way he stopped by the sail loft to say good-bye. He was surprised that Mr. Bridges was more emotional about his leaving than his mother had been. They walked to the ship together, and Mr. Bridges stood on shore while James boarded the *Royal Lewis* and stood there waving as the ship weighed anchor and moved out to the open sea. His mother had stayed home and had waved good-bye to James from the door as if he were leaving, as always, only for the day.

Powder boy on the *Royal Lewis* was the lowest and dirtiest of jobs, and James soon realized that it consisted of more than just preparing for battle. He was often called to serve meals, act as cabin boy, and do whatever else no one in particular was assigned to do. James hid his resentment behind an expressionless face and slow smile and tried especially to make himself useful to Captain Decatur. He stood by ready to serve the captain's meals, to clear the table, or to clean the captain's quarters and was soon recognized as being reserved for the service of the captain. As a result, he escaped some of the dirtier jobs.

He was eager for his first battle, and it seemed forever until the day that the cry came from the ship's lookout that the British ship *Activist* had been spotted. The quiet *Royal Lewis* became a whirl of activity as the regular privateers, in a disciplined manner, began running to their respective posts and shouting out orders. James's head was spinning. He had forgotten all he had learned. He didn't know where to start.

"James Forten," a voice called out impatiently, sounding as if it had called him many times before. "Over here!"

James ran over to the gun crew and stood in position near the powder and balls and waited, hoping that no one would notice his trembling. The *Royal Lewis* came remarkably close to the other ship, it seemed, before the voice of the British captain broke the silence.

"This is His Majesty's frigate *Activist*," he called. "What ship is that?"

Captain Decatur's answer was to signal his men to attack. Almost immediately there was a deafening roar followed by a flash of fire from the cannon, and the deck shook under James's feet. The smell of smoke filled the air and blinded him, making him cough and sneeze. He was so frightened that he froze until a sharp nudge on his shoulder reminded him of his job. By blind instinct, he began passing the powder and cannonballs to the loader, who forced them down the muzzle with a ramrod.

Now that the battle was really on, James could see the extreme danger of his job as powder boy. When the ammunition was low, James had to run below deck to the magazine for more powder and cannonballs. He would then have to run back to his post, shielding the explosive powder from the flying sparks, which could ignite an explosion fatal to him. All around him the sparks flew, forcing him to keep moving, although he had to step over the bodies of wounded, groaning men who cried out to him for help. The battle seemed to last an eternity, and both ships appeared to be utterly destroyed.

The two ships were so close now that the crew from the *Royal Lewis* began jumping over to the deck of the *Activist* to continue the battle in man-to-man combat. James, however, stayed at his post, passing powder and balls until his arms felt like rubber. The battle finally took an upward swing when the *Activist* began burning in several places and the captain was seriously wounded. Soon the British flag was lowered in surrender, and the long battle had ended at last.

The *Activist* did not have the rich cargo that James and all the crew of the *Royal Lewis* had hoped for. As James looked around at the mangled ships and the wounded and dead men on both vessels, he wondered if it had been worth it. However, it was just the first of several battles for James, and some of the later ones brought important prisoners or goods that could be exchanged for large amounts of money. But too soon their luck changed.

One day, about three months after that first battle, as the *Royal Lewis* approached a British warship called the *Amphyon*, the lookout suddenly spotted two more British vessels in the distance. Realizing the impossibility of fighting three ships at one time, the *Royal Lewis* decided to make a run for it, but the British took up the chase. Before long, they were close enough to begin firing. At the first shot, Captain Decatur immediately gave orders to strike colors. The American flag fluttered down in surrender.

It was then that James went into a complete panic. He wanted to run and scream. He knew that black sailors were never kept for prisoner exchanges but were sold into slavery in the West Indies as part of the cargo. Running below to his bunk, he had just enough time to snatch up his blanket, Bible, and marbles before he was ordered on deck by one of the British officers. The crew of the *Royal Lewis* was divided into three groups and sent to the three British ships. James was with the group taken by the *Amphyon.* As the prisoners filed past the captain, James was stopped and the captain asked sharply, "What's in that bag, boy?"

"What bag?" said James in confusion, looking down. His marbles in a small cloth sack dangled from his wrist.

"How old are you?" demanded the captain.

"Fifteen," answered James quickly, forgetting his former lie.

"I said, 'What's in that bag?'" the captain demanded again.

"Marbles," James answered, feeling very embarrassed and childish. He didn't know now what had made him bring them.

"What's your name?" asked the captain.

James figured this was the end for him. The captain probably already had a prospective buyer in mind. He stood tall and answered without faltering, "My name is James Forten."

The captain smiled and waved him on. A few hours later, while James sat with the other prisoners, a British youth with rosy cheeks, straight brown hair, and a pouting mouth approached him.

"Are you James Forten, the powder boy from the *Royal Lewis?*" he asked.

James nodded.

"I am Willie Beasley, the son of Sir John, the captain of the *Amphyon,*" he said with a heavy British accent. "My father tells me that you brought a bag of marbles on board. I'm a champion. Would you like to play a game?"

James took out his marbles with great pride now and followed Willie on deck. They placed the marbles in a group on the floor between them. At first they played seriously and silently, but soon, in boyish glee, they were laughing and teasing. James was trying to decide whether or not to let Willie Beasley win, for he was sure he couldn't be beaten. His perfect aim and strong fingers had won him the neighborhood championship for years. He decided to win first and then to let Willie win. He was surprised to find out, however, that letting Willie win was no problem because he really was very good, and James had to play carefully to beat him. It was the first of many games, and in spite of themselves, the boys became fast friends, so James was in no way treated as a prisoner. At first he thought the other prisoners would be angry, but they didn't seem to notice. Sir John was glad that Willie had met someone his own age to entertain him since the trip had turned out to be a long and boring one for the boy. During one of their long days together, Willie asked James to go back to England with him. James instantly flared.

"I'll never be a traitor!" he snapped.

"What difference does it make since you're nothing but a slave in your own country anyway?" asked Willie.

"I am not a slave!" said James angrily. "I was born free."

"Well, you're just a black prisoner now," retorted Willie. "And you have only two choices. You will either be sold as a slave, or you can come to England with me as a friend." He suddenly dropped his belligerent attitude. "Oh, come on, James," he begged. "England abolished slavery. You'll get an education and live in a beautiful home. Father likes you. He thinks you have a fine mind."

James didn't answer. He was tempted, but somehow it didn't seem right. When Sir John sent for him the next day, James stood before him and refused his offer to go to England.

"You must be a fool!" exclaimed Sir John in perplexed anger.

"I am an American prisoner," said James. "I cannot be a traitor to my country."

Willie broke in. "America is not your country, James. All you are there is a slave."

"I am not a slave," answered James, quietly this time.

"Well, all you are there, then, is a servant," said Willie. "I could understand your loyalty if you were white."

This time James didn't answer.

Sir John sighed. He had spoiled Willie by trying to give him everything he wanted. Now he hated to see him disappointed. In an effort to change James's mind, he said, "You know you'll have to be sold."

James didn't know what to say. He opened his mouth to speak, but changed his mind and said nothing.

"Well?" asked Willie.

"I cannot be a traitor," James answered. Lifting his dark pain-filled eyes and looking directly at Willie, he almost whispered, "I never want to be a slave." He turned and quickly left.

The next day before the prisoner exchange, Willie Beasley approached James.

"You will be transferred to the *Jersey* with the other prisoners," he said. As soon as he started talking, his eyes filled with tears. "It is nothing but a floating death trap. No one gets off alive." He handed James a white envelope. "This is from Father to the captain of the *Jersey*. It will help you. Goodbye, James." He turned and hurried away. Looking down at the white envelope, James realized that Willie was one of the best friends he would ever have. Somehow he knew that they would never meet again.

When James boarded the *Jersey*, he handed the white envelope to the officer in charge, who barely glanced at it and waved him on without comment. He was sent below to the main prisoner quarters, where his nostrils were immediately assailed by the loathsome odor of human filth, and all around the dark hole he could hear the ravings and groanings of the sick and dying. James knew that he was probably the only black on board. His mind went back to Mr. Benezet, his teacher, and his school lessons on how the slaves were captured and brought to America in the pits of ships. He now knew just how they must have felt. He knew why they were so submissive and broken when they were finally sold. They said that no man sentenced to the *Jersey* survived unless he was removed in a short time, but then, James thought, most prisoners were white. He thought of his great-grandfather who had survived the slave ship and of his grandfather who had bought his freedom. From the number of African slaves in America, James realized that quite a few of them must have survived, and in a sudden surge of pride, he realized that he was of the same race. He would make it, too.

When the prisoners were brought on deck the next day, James recognized Daniel Brewton, who looked gravely ill. They were glad to see each other, and because of their past association, they quickly became friends. This relationship was hard on James because Daniel was so sickly that James ended up doing chores and hustling food for both of them. Nevertheless, James was still able to volunteer for extra jobs, and in his usual manner he picked the ones that kept him on deck and out of the stinking hole as much as possible. He loaded supplies, scrubbed the deck, and even volunteered to bring up the corpses of dead prisoners. After the first few times, this task no longer bothered him. Not only did James survive, but he also grew tough.

He never knew if it was the letter Sir John had written that prompted another prisoner to seek him out one morning while he was doing his chores. The man, who was an officer, told James he was being exchanged for a British prisoner and that he was taking a trunk with him that would hold one person. Joy flooded James's heart to think that he might finally escape, but instinct warned him not to tell Daniel. Somehow he felt like a traitor leaving him behind to die. He rudely avoided Daniel the remainder of the day. That night when Daniel sought him out in the dark pit where they usually huddled together and talked about Philadelphia, their mothers and sisters, and old times, James pretended he was sleepy.

"Leave me alone, Daniel!" he snapped.

"What's wrong?" asked Daniel.

"Nothing," James snapped again. "I'm just sick and tired of waiting to get off this boat."

"I don't think I'm ever going to get off," said Daniel. "I don't think I'm ever going to see Philadelphia or my home again." His voice cracked, and James knew that he was crying.

Long after Daniel had fallen asleep, James still lay awake, hating himself for what he knew he had to do. The next morning Daniel did not even want to go up on deck for fresh air, and James had to practically carry him up. His face was gray and his eyelids were red and swollen. His body was covered with sores. His eyes seemed to be constantly pleading with James. That evening James slipped Daniel into the trunk, and the next morning he and the officer carried the trunk down to the waiting boat, which took it and the officer to freedom. As the boat disappeared toward shore, James swallowed hard and fought back the tears, knowing that it was too late to change his mind now and that a golden opportunity had slipped through his fingers.

"I can make it," he whispered to himself. "I know I can make it." He put his hand in his pocket and felt the round hardness of his bag of marbles that he had childishly clung to since leaving home. In sudden anger, he tossed them into the sea. He would never need them again. They belonged to the world of Fred and Larry, and now, Daniel. He felt like a tired old man as he turned back to the *Jersey* and wondered how he could make it through another day.

He did make it through, though. That day, and the next day, and the next—for three more months. Near the end of the war, he was freed in a general prisoner exchange. After the American ship, loaded with returning prisoners, docked in Philadelphia,

James walked down the tiny streets of his boyhood home, wondering how the houses and streets could ever have looked so huge to him. A few people glanced at him curiously, some with recognition, but he barely noticed anyone. He was thinking of his mother and wondering if she knew he was on his way. He knew that even if she did know, she wouldn't be waiting at the door but would be in the kitchen cooking and would try to pretend that his walking through the door after all this time was nothing very exciting. But the smell of biscuits and gravy would soon fill the house, and her singing voice would float from the kitchen. Long before nightfall the whole neighborhood would know that Sarah Forten's boy was home.

James pushed the door open, and the aroma of cooking food filled his nostrils. She knew. When he walked into the kitchen, she didn't even look up until he whirled her around in a bear hug. In spite of herself, she could not help crying when she saw how much James looked like his father. He was now six feet two inches and thin as a rail.

"You're so skinny," she said, shaking her head.

"They don't cook like you do on the *Jersey*," replied James, laughing. "Where is Abigail?"

"Oh, she lives down the street now," said his mother. "There was no way to tell you. She's married."

"Married!" exclaimed James. To him Abigail was just a child. He couldn't imagine her married.

"Daniel Brewton was here and told us how you slipped him off the boat," his mother said. "I'm proud of you."

She piled his plate high with rice and gravy and biscuits and pork chops and okra, just the way James had dreamed of her doing over and over again while he lay in the dark misery of the *Jersey*, counting off the passing days. It had taken 210 days for the dream to come true.

Acknowledgments *(continued from p. ii)*

Random House, Inc.
From "White Shark" by Peter Benchley. Copyright © 1994 by Peter Benchley. Reprinted by permission of Random House, Inc.

Marian Reiner
"Sea Songs" by Myra Cohn Livingston (Holiday House). Copyright © 1986 by Myra Cohn Livingston. Used by permission of Marian Reiner.

Simon & Schuster Books for Young Readers, an imprint of Simon & Schuster Children's Publishing Division
From *Call It Courage* by Armstrong Sperry is reprinted with the permission of Simon & Schuster Books for Young Readers, an imprint of Simon & Schuster Children's Publishing Division. Copyright 1940 Macmillan Publishing Company; copyright renewed © 1968 Armstong Sperry.

Note: Every effort has been made to locate the copyright owner of material reprinted in this book. Omissions brought to our attention will be corrected in subsequent editions.